Recreation and Parks
The Profession

Betty van der Smissen

HUMAN KINETICS

Library of Congress Cataloging-in-Publication Data

van der Smissen, Betty, 1927-
  Recreation and parks : the profession / Betty van der Smissen
      p. cm.
  Includes bibliographical references.
  ISBN 0-7360-4562-7 (soft cover : alk. paper)
 1. Recreation--Vocational guidance--United States.   2. Leisure--Vocational guidance--United States.   I.
Title.
  GV160.v36 2005
  790' .023'73--dc22

2005008663

ISBN: 0-7360-4562-7

The Web addresses cited in this text were current as of December 2004, unless otherwise noted.

Acquisitions Editor: Gayle Kassing, PhD
Developmental Editor: Anne Cole
Assistant Editor: Bethany Bentley
Copyeditor: Annette Pierce
Proofreader: Kathy Bennett
Graphic Designer: Robert Reuther
Graphic Artist: Kathleen Boudreau-Fuoss
Cover Designer: Keith Blomberg
Printer: Versa Press

Printed in the United States of America 10 9 8 7 6 5 4 3 2 1

Human Kinetics
Web site: www.HumanKinetics.com

United States: Human Kinetics
P.O. Box 5076, Champaign, IL 61825-5076
800-747-4457
e-mail: humank@hkusa.com

Canada: Human Kinetics
475 Devonshire Road Unit 100, Windsor, ON N8Y 2L5
800-465-7301 (in Canada only)
e-mail: orders@hkcanada.com

Europe: Human Kinetics
107 Bradford Road, Stanningley, Leeds LS28 6AT, United Kingdom
+44 (0) 113 255 5665
e-mail: hk@hkeurope.com

Australia: Human Kinetics
57A Price Avenue, Lower Mitcham, South Australia 5062
08 8277 1555
e-mail: liaw@hkaustralia.com

New Zealand: Human Kinetics
Division of Sports Distributors NZ Ltd.
P.O. Box 300 226 Albany, North Shore City, Auckland
0064 9 448 1207
e-mail: info@humankinetics.co.nz

Contents

Preface

An understanding of the recreation and parks profession is key to being a more successful professional. It enables you to gain insights into the larger field and gain a broader vision so that you can provide a higher quality of service to the community and society. Further, knowledge of professional resources allows you to better perform the tasks at hand.

An understanding of the recreation and parks profession is also key to enhancing it, which strengthens the belief among other leaders in the community and society in the profession's contribution to solving community and societal problems and enriching the quality of life of all. When a professional can articulate the nature of the profession, he or she can provide more effective leadership within the community and society.

But, the recreation and parks profession is so multifaceted that it is difficult to possess knowledge about its entire scope and its many aspects or segments. Most literature and organizations address only a selected aspect or segment. This book seeks to set forth the scope and essence of the profession in a concise manner. It endeavors to create a greater understanding of and appreciation for the profession, not only among students and young professionals, but also among leaders of the recreation and parks profession and those who are established in the profession.

The book is presented in four parts. Part I focuses on the nature of the profession, includ-ing the marks of a profession, the facets of the profession, the role of professional organizations, and starting in the profession. Part II provides a time line (1500 to 2005) of selected events in the comparative development of 15 segments of the profession. Part III categorizes the professional organizations associated with recreation and parks into six areas of focus and describes the organizations' functions and services. Part IV provides a detailed bibliography of literature and resources, organized into 12 functional sections. You can access a color version of the time line and a list of updated information for and links to the professional organizations at www.HumanKinetics.com/RecreationAndParks.

Today many academic departments and faculty, and some public agencies, embrace the term *leisure services* either to replace (believing it encompasses recreation and parks and is more broad) or to use in conjunction with recreation and parks. This book does not address the definition and philosophy of terminology (there is plenty in the literature on that topic!), but uses the term *recreation and parks* to include the scope presented in this book.

This book is not a comprehensive treatise. It provides a limited view of the scope and essence of the profession. Much more could be written, and has been written, related to any one of the segments. The recreation and park profession is both extensive and dynamic.

Acknowledgments

Every person has an obligation to enhance their profession; through such involvement you will receive professional stimulation and gratification. This book was written because of the meaning of professional organization participation to the author in an effort to make available to students and young professionals some basic information and understanding about the recreation and parks profession, as well as to share with them the importance of their involvement in professional organizations to their advancement in their career. Some individuals believe they do not have time to be involved; they do not realize the professional they could become and their responsibility to advance the profession.

Often I am asked what has given me the greatest satisfaction in my 50 years of being in education. Without a question, it is my students. I dedicate this book to my graduate assistants and my advisees, especially those with whom I've had the pleasure of working on theses and dissertations (which number well over 100). You know who you are and I appreciate how you have both enriched my life and our profession! You have made a difference in our profession by becoming scholars with your research and publications and particularly by your involvement in and contribution to the profession at all levels. A few years ago, at least 20 of you (my advisees) were elected as **national presidents** of your respective organizations and this honor comes to you only through giving a great deal of time, effort, and commitment to the profession. You are all quality individuals and have made the profession better.

I'd also like to express appreciation to the many fine professional colleagues with whom I've had the privilege of associating through professional organization activity in my fields of interest (law, camping-environmental education-adventure/challenge, and recreation).

Part I

Nature of the Profession

Many recreation and park students have been subjected to the taunt, "You mean you get paid for playing?" Or, worse yet, when a person employed in recreation and parks is asked, "What do you do?" her response, "I'm in recreation and parks," is met with an "oh" and an uncomfortable silence.

The general public, despite involvement in recreational activity and extensive use of the facilities and services of recreation and parks entities, does not seem to understand the nature of the recreation and parks profession. Does it really take a professional in recreation and parks to perform the job? Anyone can conduct activities and maintain parks, can't they? What is uniquely required? Is recreation and parks really a profession? Does it meet the criteria or *marks of a profession* that establish a field of employment as a profession?

The general public's experience with recreation and parks is through activities that take place in many different settings and recreational facilities or services. The public may not realize that the recreational activities are used as a modality or strategy to meet certain goals. Just what is the field of parks and recreation? Indeed, the field is multifaceted.

One mark of a profession is professional organization, but just what is the role of such an organization? What professional organizations are available to recreation and parks professionals, and what functions and services do they provide? Why should professionals be involved in a organization?

Whether you are a student seeking to enter the profession or an employed professional seeking advancement, you must understand how to get off to a sound start in the profession. Thus, both students and professionals must understand more fully the nature of the profession to be able to articulate its essence to the public, as well as to enhance their own professional careers.

This part sets forth four aspects that describe the nature of the parks and recreation profession:

- Marks of a profession
- A multifaceted field
- Role of professional organizations
- Starting in the profession

MARKS OF A PROFESSION

Is parks and recreation a profession? Some say no because the field is not well defined, and activities are a common tool or strategy used to meet organizational objectives. In addition, the physical settings, such as natural areas and buildings, can be managed without specific educational background in recreation and parks. Certainly you can enter the field from many different disciplines. Indeed, this question is an important topic for discussion. The following criteria will help us examine the question objectively and show why recreation and parks is a profession.

In order for a career field to be classified as a profession, it must meet certain criteria, called *marks of a profession*. The following are the five marks of a profession:

1. A unique body of knowledge
2. Applied and basic research
3. Professional literature

4. Accreditation
5. Professional organization

When these are applied to recreation and parks, the answer must be yes, parks and recreation *is* a profession!

Unique Body of Knowledge

Because recreation and parks is a multifaceted field, it has many disciplinary antecedents. Within these disciplines (historically evidenced in the comparative time line, part II) we can find the body of knowledge. The antecedent disciplines may be broadly categorized into five areas: natural environment, management, behavioral sciences (human social development), human welfare (social problems), and therapy and medicine (human physical development). See figure 1.1.

Urban and rural parks planning, development, and management come out of the natural environment disciplines, especially forestry, horticulture, and landscape

---

Natural Environment

Forestry
Landscape Architecture
Biological and Natural Sciences
Geography

Management

Business
Public Administration

Behavioral Sciences

Sociology
Psychology
Anthropology
Law
Economics
Education

Human Welfare

Social Work

Therapy and Medicine

Medicine and Education
Rehabilitation
Activity Therapies (such as occupational therapy and physical therapy)
Exercise Science (including physiology and kinesiology)
Physical Education (including sport, dance, movement, and child development)

Note: This is an illustrative list, not inclusive.

FIGURE 1.1   Disciplinary antecedents.

architecture. This is particularly true in city planning. Naturalists and interpreters usually had a background in biology or natural sciences, although some had a background in geography.

The use of recreational activities as part of the modality for human social development for all ages has long been a part of voluntary associations, churches, schools, and public recreation agencies. The leadership initially came from behavioral sciences such as education, sociology, and psychology. Leisure generally has not been considered a separate behavioral science but integral to other behavioral disciplines, especially sociology.

The human welfare antecedents, such as social work, have extensively used recreational activity to address social problems and concerns, particularly in the urban setting.

Physical development, health, and rehabilitation, too, have a long history of using recreational activity (see the time line in part II). The therapy and medicine disciplines that have used activity as a modality include medicine, the various activity therapies, and physical education, including exercise science and child development.

A fifth discipline could be added: management and business. This has been a long-standing antecedent, but has recently evolved in new directions. For many years, a patronage system was used to employ recreation leaders, park workers, and administrative personnel in public recreation and parks, and therefore, a professional background in a particular discipline was not required. More recently, however, with the increased importance of effective management, including financial and legal aspects, the field of management (public administration and business) has become an important antecedent.

While recreation and parks continues to utilize these disciplines, today the field utilizes the related disciplines uniquely to its own ends, rather than the other way around. One must first understand the field of recreation and parks and its basic concepts. The focus is on and *begins with* recreation and parks, rather than recreation being used as a *setting* for behavioral research, education, or social welfare, or the recreational activity as the modality for therapy for illness or to address social concerns. Also, people expect local government to provide and maintain natural areas for public relaxation and enjoyment.

Recreation and parks requires an integration of knowledge from many disciplines with unique applications. This produces a unique body of knowledge, which professionals should have the capability (knowledge, understanding, application) to apply while managing, conducting, and administering recreation and parks in a chosen setting. Today the academic curricula include course work in the various disciplines, depending on each student's career focus; however, the professional recreation and parks courses direct the application to the field of recreation and parks. It is the ability to take a convergent knowledge base from the underlying disciplines of the profession and convert it into specialized professional practice that is tailored to the unique requirements of the clientele and provider that gives the special body of knowledge to the recreation and parks profession, or any other profession. For further discussion on this topic, see Schein and Kommers (1972) and Edginton et al. (2004).

Applied and Basic Research

A second mark of a profession is applied and basic research that professionals conduct, which they publish in recognized journals (see Selected Professional Resources, part IV) both specific to recreation and parks and to the related disciplines. The majority of recreation and parks basic research is conducted in educational institutions by individual faculty and institutes or centers and financially supported by government grants and private funding from foundations and industry. However, certain federal agencies, such as the National Park Service, the U.S. Forest Service, and the U.S. Army Corps of Engineers, conduct recreation-related basic research and provide research grants, primarily in areas related to the outdoors, health (Centers for Disease Control), and human services (e.g., youth at risk).

Applied research occurs especially with local governments, agencies, and institutions. One category (10.0) of the Commission for Accreditation of Park and Recreation Agencies (CAPRA) standards is evaluation and research, which requires a systematic evaluation program (standard 10.1) and demonstration projects and action research (standard 10.2). In addition, standards in other categories provide for evaluative research, such as trends analysis (2.1), community study (2.4.1.1), needs index (2.4.1.3), marketing research (3.3.4.2), program evaluation (6.9), and risk analysis (9.4).

Further, the National Recreation and Parks Association (NRPA) benefits movement (or program) calls for measurement of the various benefits. Also, many local organizations that receive funding from United Way are required to measure outcomes for their programs. Nearly all grants, regardless of source, require that objectives be measured to determine to what extent they have been met.

Professionals in related disciplines conduct considerable research using a recreation setting or recreational activity or both as the modality. This research is reported in their respective research journals.

Professional Literature

Research publications and literature enhance the recreation and parks profession. Most of the professional organizations produce a monthly professional periodical and a newsletter, as well as conference and workshop proceedings, and often other publications of how best to do something (e.g., "best practices"). See part III for publications of the respective organizations. In addition, a considerable body of literature presents the various facets of the profession and operational practices. See part IV for selected resources.

Accreditation

Accreditation is the assessment of the degree to which an institution, agency, or program meets the standards set forth by the profession—the desired professional practices. *Self-Assessment Manual for Quality Operation of Park and Recreation Agencies,* published in 2001 by the Commission for Accreditation of Park and Recreation Agencies (CAPRA), discusses standards. "A standard is a statement of desirable practice as set forth by experienced and recognized professionals. . . . Standards enable evaluation by comparison—comparing what is within an agency operation with what is accepted by professionals as desirable." (xiii)

Four commonalities exist among accreditation systems:

- Standards. The standards for the various accreditation systems were developed by professionals and are updated periodically. The agency seeking accreditation may be required to meet a certain percentage of the standards and may be mandated to meet designated standards. Each standard is composed of three parts: (a) the standard itself; (b) interpretation of the standard to help the agency seeking accreditation better understand the terminology and intent of the standard; and (c) evidence of compliance.

• Self-assessment. One of the greatest values of accreditation is in the required self-assessment. How well does the agency say its practices meet each standard? Are the standards in compliance?

• Visitation team. After the self-assessment, a team of peers from the profession visits the agency to verify compliance. The team members usually have had special training in interpretation of the standards and how to verify compliance. The team does not determine whether an agency is accredited, but reports its compliance findings to a council, commission, or board.

• Council, commission, or board. This is the entity that reviews the agency's self-assessment and the team's compliance report and, often after a hearing at which it can ask questions of the agency seeking accreditation, determines whether the agency is to be accredited.

The parks and recreation profession recognizes two types of accreditation: academic curriculum accreditation and agency or program accreditation (see part III, page 97 in the section on Certifying and Accrediting Agencies and Academies; see also van der Smissen 2004).

Why be accredited? Accreditation is fundamental for protection of the public. It represents a *minimum* compliance with certain standards. Accreditation is not restrictive, but rather a way to benchmark quality practices for a profession. Thus, accreditation is considered one of the marks of a profession.

"The reason it took so long for the academic curriculum accreditation to be recognized by the Commission on Postsecondary Accreditation (COPA) is because the Council could not document satisfactorily how curriculum accreditation was essential to protect the public, those who would hire the graduates and conduct the park and recreation services. CAPRA accreditation is an indicator to the public, the agency's constituency, regarding the quality of operation and thus protects the public not only in the nature of the programs/services provided, but also in management accountability, such as fiscal accountability and physical resource conservation. Camp accreditation is to give an indicator of the quality of camps to the public in selecting a camp for children to attend. Adventure program accreditation gives some assurance as to the safety and program practices not only to those who would send children to such programs, but also to agencies, such as serve youth-at-risk and use adventure/challenge activities as part of their treatment program or schools that want to include adventure programs in their curriculum, and that seek to contract with an adventure program operator." (van der Smissen 2004, 12–13)

For academic institutions, curriculum accreditation was established to provide coherence to park and recreation curricula. Students planning to major in recreation and parks know that in any accredited curriculum, regardless of state or type of institution, a certain basic educational foundation core will be used to support an in-depth specialization or a professional career focus. Employers, whether public, nonprofit, or commercial, know that a recreation and parks student has a basic foundation in the recreation and parks field. Just as medical or law schools are accredited to assure the public that a graduating physician or lawyer has a certain level of competence, so it is with the recreation and parks field.

Academic Accreditation

The Council for Higher Education Accreditation (CHEA)—formerly COPA—is an organization of college and university presidents that approves organizations seeking to come on campus to accredit an academic program. The Council on Accreditation (COA) for recreation and park, jointly sponsored by NRPA and American Association for Physical Activity and Recreation (AAPAR—formerly AALR), is approved, as is the National Council for Accreditation of Teacher Education (NCATE), which accredits physical education and sometimes recreation, and the regional accrediting agencies, which accredit higher education institutions.

Agency or Program Accreditation

Several types of agencies or programs can attain national accreditation in recreation and parks. The accreditations focus on particular agencies that provide particular services. The three primary accreditations are: accreditation of recreation and parks agencies by CAPRA, accreditation of organized camps by the American Camping Association (ACA), and accreditation of adventure programs by the Association of Experiential Education (AEE). Zoos also have a national accreditation program.

Accreditation should be distinguished from licensing. Accreditation stems from a profession, while licensing is a function of government

Professional Organization

Professional organization is the fifth mark of a profession. Individuals engaged in recreation and parks have organized themselves for their mutual benefit. The comparative time line in part II identifies when recreation and parks professionals felt the need for such organization by indicating the dates that various professional organizations were founded. Many professional organizations serve the multifaceted field of recreation and parks.

A professional organization should provide nine functions or benefits to its members to enhance the profession. Most of the previous marks of a profession are embodied in the functions and benefits and are facilitated by the organization. See the section, Role of Professional Organizations, on page 10 for further description of these functions.

A MULTIFACETED FIELD

Because the recreation and parks field uses diverse recreational activities as a modality in many settings and provides various types of areas, facilities, and services also in different settings, it is indeed multifaceted. Each facet is provided by a different entity that applies its own objectives and operational philosophy, and therefore, each facet exhibits distinguishing characteristics (see table 1.1). Students and professionals should be aware of this great diversity and respect the unique role and contribution of each provider, as well as the specific knowledge, understanding, abilities, and skills each requires.

Providers

Twelve different entities, or providers, are set forth in table 1.1. They can be divided into five categories. The first two relate to a public entity (city and county) as a

TABLE 1.1 Facets of the Park and Recreation Field by Provider

	Provider	Focus audience	Primary funding source	Operational philosophy	Resource vs. people emphasis	Historical leadership	Education[1]	Accreditation/ certification[2]	Use of volunteers	Use of promotion	To whom responsible
Public entity	Public recreation: parks division	Everyone in jurisdiction	Government funded/user fees/ taxes	Environmental quality for use of people	Resource	Forestry/ landscape architecture	Parks and natural resource management	CPRA	Limited	General publicity only	Elected governing body
	Public recreation: recreation division	Everyone	Government funded/user fees, some entitlements	Human services	People	Social work/ physical education	Recreation management	CPRA	Limited	General information only	Elected governing body
Special need/ membership oriented	Private non-profit (special need; community-oriented)	Groups in need	Donations, some service fees, entitlements, United Way	Human services/ quality of life	People	Social work	Program management and social work	None	Extensive	Limited	Board of directors (self-perpetuating)
	Hospitals (institution-oriented)	Special populations	Patient fees (insurance, third party)	Prescriptive and rehabilitative	People	Rehabilitation & therapies	Therapeutic recreation	NCTRC	Yes	No	Hospital administration
	Nonprofit/ voluntary agencies	Members of organization, but open to community	Membership and user fees, donations, United Way Fund, fund raisers	Human services/ quality of life	People	Social work/ physical education	Recreation management	None	Yes	Limited	Membership elects board of directors
	Private clubs (golf, health)	Community clientele	Members, user fees, services	Specialized service/quality of life	People	Business, fitness specialists	Commercial recreation	May be specialized— fitness, golf pro	No	Membership recruitment	Ownership or membership
Commercial recreation/ tourism	Commercial recreation and tourism	Specific target audience	User fees	Marketing and individualistic profit	People and resources	Business	Commercial recreation and tourism management	None	No	Yes, extensive advertising	Financial base (stockholders, customers, owner)
Closed groups	Employee recreation	Employees of companies	Company benefit, employee organization	Quality of life, productivity, health care costs	People	Personnel	Recreation and fitness management	Fitness	No	No	Company
	Campus recreation (college)	Students	Student activity fees; user club fees	Enrichment of life	People	Physical education	Recreation and fitness management	Intramurals	No	Limited	Student affairs office, university/ college administration
	Church recreation	Members of church	Donations, members, rentals	Quality of life	People	Ministry	Recreation management	None	Yes	No	Church governance
	Prison recreation	Inmates	Government funded or contract	Human services/ quality of life	People	Personnel	Recreation and fitness management	None	Limited	No	Prison hierarchy, government
	Military recreation	Military personnel	Government funded, auxiliary enterprise	Human services/ quality of life	People	Personnel	Recreation and fitness management	None	Limited	No	Military hierarchy, federal government

Note: These are generalized characteristics to assist in noting differences and similarities among providers.

[1] Only as related to Park, Recreation, and Tourism curriculum.

[2] Only those for the professional group as a whole (see Part III Professional Organizations for specific certifications offered).

provider, but are presented separately because of their separate historical development of *parks* as part of city planning and *recreation* as a social service (see the time line in part II).

The next two providers encompass special-need populations. Private nonprofit providers direct their services to individuals with special needs, as under the Americans with Disabilities Act of 1990, and to others with special needs, such as youth at risk and seniors, primarily in community-oriented settings. The second special-need provider, hospitals, uses an institution-oriented setting to provide services based on therapeutic prescriptives and physical and mental health.

The two membership-oriented providers, private nonprofit associations and private clubs, exhibit quite different characteristics than the other providers. Private nonprofit associations encompass the voluntary associations with open public membership. They direct their attention toward human services. Private clubs usually are concerned with specific services, such as golf or fitness, and membership is available to those who pay for the services of the club.

A large number of providers fall into the next category of commercial recreation and tourism. These are usually small businesses and are not membership based, but are customer oriented with profit-making services for those willing to buy the service.

The last five entities are providers to closed groups, serving only their own constituency: company employees; college students, faculty, and staff; church members and its outreach; prisoners; and members of the military and their families.

It should be noted that utilization of recreation activity and service is essential and integral for all providers, regardless of whether they are public, nonprofit, or commercial. This commonality makes them a facet in the park and recreation field.

Characteristics

Twelve characteristics are generalized to help you note the differences and similarities among the providers.

- Focus audience. To whom is the service primarily directed: to the public at large as customers or to a target audience, such as a special population or closed eligibility or membership (e.g., prisons)?
- Primary funding source. What is the basic source of financial support: taxes, user fees and charges, membership dues, donations, or sponsoring entity?
- Operational philosophy. What is the underlying organizational goal or focus: the natural environment, human services, financial profit, health-oriented, prescription, or quality of life?
- Emphasis. Is the provider more focused on the resource (natural environment), or on service to people?
- Historical leadership. What are the antecedent disciplines?
- Education. What type of academic background related to the recreation and parks area is required?
- Accreditation/certification. Is agency accreditation or professional certification available?
- Use of volunteers. To what extent are volunteers used?
- Use of promotion. To what extent are programs and services marketed?
- To whom responsible. What is the primary authority that controls the provider?

ROLE OF PROFESSIONAL ORGANIZATIONS

Recreation and park organizations can be grouped into four categories: special interest organizations, trade associations, related professional organizations, and professional organizations with a primary focus on the recreation and parks field. See figure 1.2 for examples. Many organizations exist, especially in the first three categories. Columbia Books annually issues two companion directories, *National Trade and Professional Associations of the United States*, which provides basic information on approximately 7,600 associations, and *State and Regional Associations of the United States*, also listing approximately 7,500 associations.

Special interest organizations can be separated into two categories. One type of organization focuses on a specific activity (e.g., canoeing, bicycling, or hiking) that individual members participate in. The second type of organization, support organizations, advance a special interest (e.g., Sierra Club or National Audubon Society). Membership is open to anyone interested in the specific interest or focus. Many of these organizations were established many years ago (see time line in part II).

Trade associations are established by the commercial leisure industry to advance the industry. Examples of trade associations include campgrounds, health and sports clubs, and paddle sports. They provide conferences and resource materials and work with legislative bodies and product suppliers for the good of the industry.

Organizations of related professions fall into two areas. The first is professional organizations for people performing a specific function utilized in the recreation and park field, for example, marketing and the American Marketing Association (AMA). The second type of organization utilizes recreation within its profession and provides a special section within the organization, such as the American Sociological Association's (ASA) section on sociology of leisure or the Society of American Foresters (SAF), which has created a recreation working group.

The fourth type of organization is the professional organizations primarily focused on the recreation and parks field. Recreation and parks is a multifaceted field that includes many professional organizations. However, the organizations do not directly parallel the facets. These organizations have three approaches:

• An umbrella organization. This has organization branches or associations, such as the National Recreation and Parks Association (NRPA) and the American Alliance for Health, Physical Education, Recreation and Dance (AAHPERD).

• A particular program service, such as interpretative services and adventure and challenge programs, with subsections that provide services in a particular setting, such as schools and colleges, zoos, and therapeutic settings. Examples of this approach include the National Association for Interpretation (NAI), the Association for Experiential Education (AEE), and the American Camping Association (ACA).

• Single-focus organizations. For example, the North American Association for Environmental Education (NAAEE) focuses on environmental education, the Travel and Tourism Research Association (TTRA) focuses on tourism, and the Sport and Recreation Law Association (SRLA) focuses on legal aspects of the field. See part III for a complete list of organizations and subunits.

Table 1.1 categorizes organizations by 12 providers, while this part and part III separate the organizations into five categories of professional organizations specific to the recreation and parks field: recreation, outdoor programming, parks/natural

Special Interest

Focus on an activity

        Canoeing: American Canoe Association (ACA)
        Hiking: Appalachian Mountain Club (AMC)
        Bicycling: National Off-Road Bicycle Association (NOBA)
        Archery: National Archery Association (NAA)
        Skiing: U.S. Ski Association (USSA)
        Firearms: National Rifle Association (NRA)

Support organizations

        Environment: National Audubon Society
        Environment: Sierra Club
        Youth sports: National Alliance for Youth Sports (NAYS)

Trade Associations

Campgrounds: National Association of RV Parks and Campgrounds (NARVPC)
Amusement parks: International Association of Amusement Parks and Attractions (IAAPA)
Health and sport clubs: International Health, Racquet & Sportsclub Association (IHRSA)
Paddle sports: Professional Paddlesports Association (PPA)

Related Professional Organizations

Similar functions performed by individuals in professional organizations

        Marketing
        Public relations
        Legal counsel
        Advertising
        Accounting
        Planning
        Risk management
        Financial management
        Human resources (personnel)
        Nursing
        Athletic training

Organizations that utilize recreation and park services or are involved with the field

        Society of American Foresters (SAF)
        American Sociological Association (ASA)

Professional Organizations Focused on Recreation and Parks

(The following organizations are detailed in part III)

Umbrella organizations
        National Recreation and Parks Association (NRPA)
        American Alliance for Health, Physical Education, Recreation and Dance (AAHPERD)

Organizations that provide a particular program or service
        National Association for Interpretation (NAI)
        Association for Experiential Education (AEE)
        American Camping Association (ACA)

Single-focus organizations
        North American Association for Environmental Education (NAAEE)
        Travel and Tourism Research Association (TTRA)
        Sport and Recreation Law Association (SRLA)

FIGURE 1.2   **Types of organizations.**

resources, private/commercial and tourism, and therapeutic recreation, disabilities, and fitness.

Those organizations directed toward providing recreation programs in public entities, such as schools, the military, and cities and counties, are in the recreation category, while public entities dealing with natural resources are in the category natural resources. Outdoor and therapeutic recreation program-focused organizations are categorized in their respective focus. See figure 1.3 for a list of the organizations in each category. The branches of NRPA and councils of the AAHPERD are listed in the appropriate category. Detailed information about each organization is included in part III.

Functions

A professional organization should provide nine functions or benefits to its members to enhance the profession. See part III for the specific functions for each organization.

- Opportunities for networking. One of the principal functions of a professional organization is to provide an opportunity for its members to get to know their professional colleagues and to share ideas about the profession and its conduct. This may come through formal gatherings, such as conferences and workshops, or through Internet and phone contacts and informal conversations.

- Ethics code. A profession usually adopts an ethics code by which its members conduct themselves. NRPA has an overall recreation and parks ethics code and various organizations have also developed codes for their members. See part III for specifics.

- Accreditation of programs and agencies. A program of accreditation can be developed and administered through a professional organization. (See previous section on Accreditation and part III, page 97.)

- Publications and dissemination of information. Publications and dissemination of information can come through various media, such as printed materials, Internet, and videos. (See the section on Professional Literature.)

- Certification and in-service education. Licensure and certification should be distinguished. Licensure is a function of government, authorizing an individual to practice a profession (e.g., teachers, doctors, nurses, lawyers); few states license recreation and parks personnel. Certification is a function of the profession or related organization. Certification is recognition that a person has met certain competency requirements to perform a certain function or task. Three types of certification are overall professional certification, certification of skill-oriented competencies, and certification for completion of a designated educational program.

For the individual professional, certification is a job credential, telling the employer and clientele that your training has been recognized by the sponsoring agency. Certification is also a way for professional organizations to promote professional training and development. Professionals must obtain the basic certification requirements, and to retain the certification, they must be engaged in continuing education by acquiring continuing education units (CEUs) or additional hours of training. It must be emphasized that a certificate is evidence only of having satisfactorily completed certain requirements. It does not guarantee that a person will act in a certain manner on the job.

Recreation

AAHPERD: American Alliance for Health, Physical Education, Recreation and Dance

AAPAR (American Association for Physical Activity and Recreation)

ACUI: Association of College Unions International

AFRS: Armed Forces Recreation Society (branch of NRPA)

APRS: American Park and Recreation Society (branch of NRPA)

CAHPERD: Canadian Association for Health, Physical Education, Recreation and Dance

CALS: Canadian Association of Leisure Studies

CIRA Ontario: Canadian Intramural Recreation Association of Ontario

CPRA: Canadian Parks and Recreation Association

NASSM: North American Society for Sport Management

NIRSA: National Intramural-Recreation Sport Association

NOHSE: National Organization for Human Service Education

NRPA: National Recreation and Parks Association

SNPO: Society for Nonprofit Organizations

SPRE: Society of Park and Recreation Educators (branch of NRPA)

WLA: World Leisure Association

Natural Resources

ARVC: National Association of RV Parks and Campgrounds

AZA: American Zoo and Aquarium Association

IFPRA: International Federation of Park & Recreation Administration

NARRP: National Association of Recreation Resource Planners

NSPR: National Society for Park Resources (branch of NRPA)

PLEA: Park Law Enforcement Association

Outdoor Programming

Includes organized camping, adventure and challenge, and environmental education, as well as interpretation

ACA: American Camping Association

ACCT: Association for Challenge Course Technology

AEE: Association for Experiential Education

ANCA: Association of Nature Center Administrators

ANSS: American Nature Study Society

AORE: Association of Outdoor Recreation and Education

ASTA: American Society of Travel Agents

CAOER: Council on Adventure and Outdoor Education/Recreation (AAHPERD)

CCA: Canadian Camping Association

CCI: Christian Camping, International

CEO: Coalition for Education in the Outdoors

Interpretation Canada

NAAEE: North American Association for Environmental Education

NAI: National Association for Interpretation

VSA: Visitor Studies Association

WEA: Wilderness Education Association

(continued)

FIGURE 1.3   Categories for park and recreation professional organizations.

Commercial Recreation and Tourism

ARVC: National Association of RV Parks and Campgrounds

ATTT: Association of Tourism Teachers and Trainers

CRTS: Commercial Recreation and Tourism Section (branch of NRPA)

ESM Association: Employee Services Management Association

IAAM: International Association of Assembly Managers

IAAPA: International Association of Amusement Parks and Attractions

IACVB: International Association of Convention and Visitor Bureaus

IFEA: International Festivals & Events Association

IHRSA: International Health, Racquet and Sportsclub Association

ISTTE: International Society of Travel & Tourism Educators

MPI: Meeting Professionals International

NASSM: North American Society for Sport Management

PPA: Professional Paddlesports Association

RCRA: Resort and Commercial Recreation Association

TTRA: Travel and Tourism Research Association

Therapeutic Recreation, Disabilities, and Fitness

ACSM: American College of Sports Medicine

ATRA: American Therapeutic Recreation Association

CTRA: Canadian Therapeutic Recreation Association

IFAPA: International Federation of Adapted Physical Activity

IHRSA: International Health, Racquet and Sportsclub Association

NAAP: National Association of Activity Professionals

NTRS: National Therapeutic Recreation Society (branch of NRPA)

FIGURE 1.3   (continued)

Certified Park and Recreation Professional (CPRP) is an overall certification sponsored by the NRPA and administered by its state affiliates. There are other professional certifications, such as for interpreters administered by the National Association for Interpretation (NAI) and for those in intramurals administered by the National Intramural-Recreational Sports Association (NIRSA). See part III for certifications by individual professional organizations. CEUs usually are required for keeping the certification current.

Organizations offer many specific skill-oriented certifications, such as CPR and first aid, lifeguarding, and various instructor certifications, such as aerobics, archery, and playground inspector. These may be offered by either professional (see part III) or specialized organizations. Skill-oriented certifications, such as first aid and lifesaving, require refresher renewals rather than CEUs. Professional certificates offered by a professional organization are different from certificates given for completing a workshop or certificates designated by educational institutions for students taking a certain selection of courses focused in a specific area.

Integral to professional enhancement is in-service education. This may occur at professional organization conferences during the educational sessions or through workshops and clinics. Other in-service opportunities include short courses and workshops made available by educational institutions and other related associations and agencies, such as Councils of Social Agencies and associated youth agencies, which vary by locale. The organization offering the educational program and the profession as a whole share responsibility for the quality of the in-service program.

In-service offerings may be formalized into CEUs. To qualify for CEU status, the presenter must complete a form for the educational session or workshop, setting forth the objectives and content, and submit it to the sponsoring organization, which usually has a committee that approves these sessions. The instructor must be qualified to offer the content.

For further discussion of certification, see the December 2002 issue of *Fitness Management.*

• Recognition of outstanding members. Most professional organizations have a program of recognition and awards. See part III for awards specific to each organization.

• Enhancement of the body of knowledge. A professional organization assists in distributing research and desirable practices related to its body of knowledge in various ways, such as at conferences and symposia, and through publications.

• Public relations. A professional organization seeks to enhance the image of the profession through the media and in other ways. Coordinated organizational efforts, particularly through statewide and national organizations, can have a greater influence on the public.

• Keeping members informed. A professional organization is the watchdog for the profession by making itself aware of possible legislation and societal concerns, not only informing members of these concerns, but also organizing them for necessary action.

Why Be a Member of a Professional Organization?

Professional organizations enable individuals to do things collectively that cannot be done as easily (or often not at all) individually. Specifically, here are seven reasons to be a member of a professional organization:

1. To share information through networking
2. To have an impact on society in a positive way and enhance your professional field, first by communicating to the public the essence of the profession and its service, and second, by influencing legislation related to the profession, its conduct, and its service, in both the broad and specific context
3. To be informed about happenings and resources such as legislation, job openings, books, workshops, and institutes that pertain to the profession, its conduct, and its services
4. To financially facilitate the services the organization provides
5. To use workshops and other educational resources to enhance the quality of in-service to handle the operational challenges of the organization
6. To advance the profession through research and other professional projects to increase the quality, depth, and understanding of practices within the field
7. To provide leadership to and influence the direction and quality of your profession

Participation

Not all recreation and parks professionals consistently and continuously participate in an organization's activities. Too many people reap the benefits of an organization without contributing even by membership or conference attendance. The greatest value of membership is not measurable by a specific product such as publications or conference discounts, but by the opportunities to network and the influence and power of the aggregate body for the good of the whole.

Participation is a way to enhance personal performance as well as the reputation of the profession in society, thus providing opportunities for participants to gain monetary benefits and greater community respect. It also provides a mechanism for contributing to your profession, thereby eliminating the temptation to be a parasite, enjoying the benefits without making a positive contribution.

The nature and extent of your commitment to an organization will vary over time, depending on your stage in the profession, the amount of administrative support in your local situation, such as time allowed and travel funds, and your particular interests. Usually, one does not sustain the same level of involvement across a career, but will cycle through various levels of emphasis. You may be very involved in a leadership role while chairing a project or committee or serving as an officer or member of a board, then perhaps play a supporting role as a committee participant or attend or present at conferences.

Leadership

A profession is built, maintained, and moved forward through the leadership and commitment of individuals. The leadership of a profession is most evident in its professional organization; all professional organizations have key leaders. The nature of the profession and what it means for a person to contribute to the profession can best be understood and appreciated by looking at the individuals who have provided this leadership to the profession.

Who are some of the leaders in the recreation and parks profession? A good source for this information is to look at the membership of the professional academies. Present academy members elect professionals who have met the specific academy criteria for membership. Each year since 1981, a series of audiotapes and videotapes of interviews with leaders in the profession has been recorded. As of 2005, 68 leaders had been interviewed (see figure 1.4).

The interviews record the leader's personal background, professional insights, advice, and philosophical beliefs. These interviews provide both the inspiration to become a leader of a professional organization and the understanding of what it means to be a contributing member of the profession. Each tape is approximately 45 minutes long. The tapes are available for loan or purchase. For more information, contact the executive director/treasurer of the academy (for contact information see part III, page 109).

Another source to identify leaders who have made a special contribution to the profession is by checking the list of award recipients for a particular organization. Of course, organizations' officers, board members, and committee members also represent current leadership figures.

(2002)

Horace Albright	Ray Freeman	Tony A. Mobley
Edith Ball	Clifton E. French	William Penn Mott, Jr.
Joseph Bannon	Geoffrey Godbey	Ernest Nance
William Bird	David E. Gray	Charles H. Odegaard
Herbert Brantley	Mary E. Grogan	Joseph O'Neill
Roger K.Brown	Robert J. Hall	Ellen O' Sullivan
Reynold Carlson	Charles E. Hartsoe	Rhodell Owens
James Colley	Donald Henkel	James A. Peterson
Robert W. Crawford	John P. Hewitt	Michael S. "Mick" Pope
Ralph S. Cryder	Thomas I. Hines	Joseph Prendergast
Joseph E. Curtis	Ford W. Hughes	Bob Robertson
John H. Davis	Ira J. Hutchison	H. Douglas Sessoms
Theodore Deppe	Walter C. Johnson	Kenneth J. Smithee
Pauline des Granges	Donald Jolley	James S. Stevens, Jr.
Russell Dickenson	O-Joong Kim	Willard C. Sutherland
Charles E. Doell	Ray L. Kisiah	R. Dean Tice
Joe Doud	Ed Koenemann	Robert F. Toalson
Newton Drury	Kathryn Krieg	Richard Trudeau
Garrett Eppley	David O. Laidlaw	James J. Truncer
Robert D. Espeseth	Janet MacLean	Joseph J. Truncer
Robert Frazer	Olga Madar	Louis F. Twardzik
Bill Frederickson	Fran Mainella	Stewart Udall

FIGURE 1.4   American Academy for Parks and Recreation Administration tape inventory.

STARTING IN THE PROFESSION

Students are interested in career opportunities within their profession and how to become a professional. Students may take four actions to lay a professional foundation.

Get Experience

- Volunteer in an agency, institution, or organization to assist in their programs; volunteer for different types of programs and with various age groups and types of participants, e.g., youth at risk and people with disabilities.
- Work part-time during the school year and full-time in the summer at jobs that will improve your credentials and help you obtain a professional position upon graduation.
- Select an internship with an agency and type of position that will provide experience in your selected career direction.

Show Professionalism

- Become a familiar face among professionals in the field.
- Become a student member of a professional organization in order to receive the organization's newsletters, magazines, and electronic correspondence, and information regarding the organization's activities.
- Become involved in the profession by attending local, state, regional, national, and international conferences and workshops. You will be able to do the following:
  - Network: As you meet the people who hire and they meet you, you become a face with a name.
  - Seek to participate on the conference program and serve on committees.
  - Volunteer to work as a room host or at registration; often you will receive free registration or a reduced registration fee.
  - Visit the job mart if there is one so you can see what types of positions are available.
  - Look over the program to see who is there and what they're presenting, attend sessions in which you are particularly interested, and meet people with similar interests.
  - Meet the officers and board members.

Be Informed

Learn as much as you can about the profession, not just about the skills and knowledge of professional practice. All of these suggestions will assist you in being informed. Observe, participate, ask questions, and read widely; others will note your professionalism!

Obtain Certifications

Many certifications are available in recreation and parks (see part III, page 97). If there is a desirable certification in your professional area of interest, plan to meet its requirements and obtain it. This not only will enhance your professional skills and knowledge, but perhaps more important, also enable you to maintain contact with other professionals with similar interests.

Part II

Comparative Time Line

Part II includes a chronological time line of historical events in the park and recreation movement. As indicated in part I, the recreation and parks field is multifaceted. A comparative time line is useful to better understand the parallel and sequential development of these facets. Most literature presents either (a) only one facet, such as general recreation, therapeutic recreation, parks, or sports, or (b) a running chronology with a mixture of facets and societal events. Part II comparatively depicts the facets across time, each distinguished with its own category.

CATEGORIES

The time line is divided into 15 categories, which are laid out vertically down the left side of the time line. For the most part, these categories parallel the providers in table 1.1. However, because of the developmental nature of these facets, the categories differ slightly. To more easily compare the historical development, think of the categories as four groupings:

- Group A: Recreation
- Group B: Outdoor programming
- Group C: Parks/natural resources
- Group D: Private/commercial and tourism

The events are not placed in exclusive categories. To help understand how the events are related and to gain a more complete picture of the history, compare the events in several categories. For example, compare the events in organized camping and the events in the nonprofit sector category.

Recreation

The recreation group represents what traditionally has been known as recreation, with focus on the use of recreational activity as a modality with people (see table 1.1, Operational Philosophy and Emphasis columns). The recreation group includes six categories: recreation, schools, organized sport (athletics), religious, nonprofit sector, and therapeutic. The recreation category includes general recreation/leisure activities and services provided primarily by public entities, including public recreation, the cultural arts, and the aspect of the military that provides recreation for the armed forces. However, the historical development of leisure, as its own entity, is not included.

Recreation, physical education, and sport in the schools, as well as campus recreation and the recreation and park academic curriculum are included in the schools category. Play as a separate entity is not included. Both amateur sport (interscholastic, intercollegiate, and Olympic) and selected professional sports are included in organized sport (athletics). The fourth category, religious, encompasses church recreation—the provision for recreation by religious groups for their constituency. The nonprofit sector category includes the voluntary youth agencies and other human service agencies. Private nonprofit (special need) providers for special populations and people with disabilities, and therapeutic recreation in the clinical setting (hospitals, including the military and Veterans Administration hospitals), and inclusive recreation in the community are included in the therapeutic recreation/special-need category.

Outdoor Programming

The outdoor programming group is distinguished by two uses: (a) the use of the natural environment as a modality and setting to enhance the lives of individuals, and (b) the provision of environmental education to enhance the experience of people visiting and enjoying the natural environment. Professionals in the organized camping, environmental education, and adventure/challenge category use interpretive services.

Parks/Natural Resources

This grouping represents what traditionally has been known as *parks* and focuses on the management of the natural resources. It includes the public parks divided into three categories according to the level of government: local parks, state and provincial parks, and national parks and resource-oriented federal agencies. Because it is important to put the parks category into appropriate perspective and context, there are two additional categories: natural resources (forestry, conservation, preservation)—which has been a long-standing societal concern—and sportsmen and outdoor organizations (the use of the outdoors for various individual sports).

Private/Commercial and Tourism

This grouping encompasses selected commercial enterprises, private clubs (e.g., golf, health, and fitness), and employee recreation. The grouping also includes a separate category for tourism.

While commercial recreation and tourism have been around for many years (see time line), except for employee recreation, they were not incorporated into park and recreation curricula until the 1980s. For this reason, these categories have been included, but set out as a separate group.

EVENTS

This book focuses on the recreation and parks profession. Therefore, the events depicted in the 15 categories emphasize significant professional events and selected events particularly pertinent to the profession. To more easily compare the development of the professional organizations as related to the different facets, their founding, name changes, and merger dates are shown in italics.

This time line is not comprehensive and includes only selected events. Nor does it endeavor to place the professional events within the societal context of the times. Although it is important to place these events within the framework of what was happening at the time, this is beyond the scope of this work. Other literature endeavors to do this (see bibliographic resources for foundations of leisure and recreation in part IV). Individuals interested in a specific facet should obtain more detailed information about the historical development of that particular facet (see Resources, part IV). There are a limited number of events cited since 1990; what is historically significant is yet to be determined—add your own!

TIME INTERVALS AND DATES

Seventeen time periods from 1500 to 2005 are arranged across the top of the time line. However, the time periods are not equal intervals. Because most of the professional development has come since 1900, 10-year intervals are used for the 1900s; intervals for the 1800s depends on the extent of the historical activity. The interval prior to the 1800s (1500-1800) is a century.

This historical time line is not held out to be historical research, because there are discrepancies in some of the dates when compared to other literature. When a discrepancy was noted, effort was made to determine the correct date by consulting primary data (if easily available) and sources that were the most historically authentic, i.e., either based on historical research or documented with a primary source. However, the importance of the time line is in comparing the development of the profession and its various facets. The specific dates usually are not important in themselves and are not critical to comparative understanding; however, the approximate time, or position in history, in relation to other events is. You should look at the trend and comparative position in time.

HOW TO USE THE TIME LINE

You can refer to individual pages of the time line in this book, but the most effective way to obtain an overall visual picture of the historical comparison of the four groupings and the individual categories is to view the time line as a whole. You can access a color version of the time line online at www.HumanKinetics.com/RecreationAndParks. You should print the time line from this Web page and position it in a large matrix with the time periods positioned horizontally across the top. The categories should be positioned vertically down the left side in the following order:

Group A: Recreation

1. Recreation (general)
2. Schools
3. Organized sport (athletics)
4. Religious
5. Nonprofit sector
6. Therapeutic (recreation/special population)

Group B: Outdoor programming

7. Organized camping, environmental education, adventure/challenge
8. Interpretive services

Group C: Parks/natural resources

9. Local parks
10. State and provincial parks
11. National parks and federal agencies
12. Natural resources
13. Sportsmen and outdoor organizations

Group D: Private/commercial and tourism

14. Private and commercial
15. Tourism

If you have access to a color printer to create a color printout of the time line, you can use the color layout and see that the dispersion and concentration of color will more effectively indicate when a category started and when the greatest activity occurred. There are many ways to use the matrix for making comparisons. Here are just a few suggestions:

- Comparison of groups. First look at the groupings and compare them as a whole. For example, look at the dates for initial activity in each group. Activity in groups A (recreation) and C (parks/natural resources) occurred very early. The formal provision of services by public entities came early (in the 1500 and 1600s, setting aside public land) for group C; for group A, it was the late 1800s (1872 playground ordinance MA and 1885 Boston sand gardens). In comparison with groups A and C, group B's (outdoor programming) activity really was initiated in the late 1700s (1749 outdoor education, 1784 interpretative services). Similarly, group D evidenced commercial and private enterprises offering recreation and leisure activity in the 1700 and 1800s.

- Comparisons within groups. Within group A (recreation), the use of schools began in the 1700s and continued with greater activity in the 1800s. The use of recreation, too, had an early start. Most of the nonprofit agencies were founded in the mid-1800s and the youth organizations early in 1900s. Public recreation, however, didn't get its start until the turn of 1900 with the initiation of playgrounds.

Care of the natural environment has long been a societal concern (see group C, natural resources category), but at the same time, lands were being set aside formally for parks as a part of local city planning (1564 St. Augustine, 1634 Boston Commons). National parks came a century later (mid-1700s). Most of the initial land was set aside for national parks in the second half of the 1800s. The development of state parks followed the same time line. Many of the federal natural resource agencies also were established during this time. Sportsmen have long used the outdoors for hunting, boating, and other recreation activities, and they established common interest clubs.

- Antecedents. The time line also supports the antecedent disciplines (see figure 1.1). For example, in parks, it was the various natural resource disciplines and city planners, while for public recreation, it was the social work field and schools. The therapeutic recreation field was allied to the medical field.

- Professional organizations. Although people participated in related recreational activity, and various entities organized services for most of the categories in the very early years, professional organization were not founded, for the most part, until about 1900 (see italicized dates on time line). The forerunner of American Institute of Park Executives (AIPE), the principal parks professional organization, began in 1898, and the principal recreation professional organization, which developed into the National Recreation Association (NRA), was founded in 1906. Then in 1966, despite beginnings that were quite different, the principal parks organization (AIPE) merged with recreation's principal organization (NRA) to form National Recreation and Park Association (NRPA). This does not mean, however, that differences did not continue (see events on the time line).

		1500-1600	1601-1700	1701-1800
GROUP A: Recreation	**Recreation (general)**	**1555-1557:** Puritans outlawed a wide range of traditional leisure activities.	**Early 1600s:** New England Puritan colonies banned dice, bowling, cards, etc. & rec on Sunday. **1608:** Robert Dover attempted to counteract Puritan influence by sponsoring Cotswold's Olympick Games on his estate near Gloucestershire. **1674:** *The Complete Gamester* publ (book of rules & instructions). **1680s:** Folk dancing & singing popular.	**1760:** Public concerts held regularly in Boston. **1794:** 1st ballet regarded as serious work, *La Foret Noire,* performed in New Chestnut Theater in Philadelphia.
	Schools			**1717:** 1st college social club. **1769-1785:** Civil War curbed school rec.
	Organized sport (athletics)	**1555:** Oxford University banned football.		
	Religious		**1618:** In *Book of Sports,* James I defended Sunday sports & encouraged games & exercise; the King James Virginia law banned dancing, fiddling, card playing, hunting, & fishing on Sunday. Puritan colonies prohibited Sunday labor, travel, & rec; embraced reading & choral societies.	
	Nonprofit sector			
	Therapeutic (recreation/ special population)			**1798:** Dr. Benjamin Rush prescribes spinning, sewing, & churching for women, & gardening & cutting corn for men.

1801-1850	1851-1875	1876-1885
1812: General land office est'd.	**1872:** 1st playground ordinance, Brookline, MA.	**1885:** Boston sand gardens. *1885: Am PE Assoc founded.*
1820: Outdoor gyms opened at Harvard & Yale. **1821:** PE at Salem Latin School, MA.	**1853:** 1st required daily exercise in schools, Boston, MA.	**1885:** Medical & educational Swedish gymnastics introduced into Boston public schools & hospitals. *1885: Am Assoc for the Advancement of PE (AAAPE) founded.*
1807: Scottish settlers in Canada began annual festivals, bon spiels, at which curling began. **1839:** Abner Doubleday designed 1st baseball field & conducted 1st baseball game. **1845:** Am baseball rules modified by Alexander Cartwright. **1848:** Oldest turnverein society, Cincinnati.	**1855:** English troops stationed in Kingston, ON, credited with introducing ice hockey to Canada. **1869:** 1st intercollegiate football game; athletic clubs founded; 1st pro baseball team. **1871:** Natl Assoc of Professional Baseball Players est'd. **1874:** 1st intercollegiate track & field meet. **1874:** Tennis brought to U.S. from Bermuda.	
1843: Young Gentlemen & Ladies Relief Society of Nauvoo Mormon Church founded.	**1852:** 1st church social hall built, Salt Lake City. **1862:** Salt Lake Theater opened. **1866:** 1st vacation church school in Boston. **1875:** Mutual Improvement Assoc est'd, Mormon Church.	**1877:** Girl Friendly Society (Episcopal) est'd.
1840: Turner societies (German influence) est'd. **1844:** George Williams founded London YMCA.	**1851:** 1st YMCA est'd in Boston & Montreal. **1855:** YMCA World Organization founded. **1856:** YMCA PE dept est'd, Brooklyn. **1858:** College YMCAs, U of MI & U of VA est'd. **1860:** 1st Boys' Club opened, Hartford, CT. **1864:** 1st Girls Club opened, Waterbury, CT. **1866:** 1st est'd settlement house began in NYC. **1870:** 1st YWCA est'd in St. John's, NB, Canada. **1874:** 1st YWCA, Philadelphia, vacation project or camp for "tired young women, drudgery for wages."	**1880:** Salvation Army started in U.S.
1815: Paper by Thomas Addy brought about 1st mental hospital. **1822:** Amusement for patients at McLean Hospital, Waverly, NY. **1840:** Henrik Ling's *Theory and Practice of Medical Gymnastics* publ; Central Institute of Gymnastics in Sweden was well est'd as academic center for training in medical gymnastics. **1850:** Florence Nightingale provided rec huts.	**1863:** Red Cross founded in Geneva, Switzerland. *1873: Intl Fed of Adapted Physical Activity founded in Quebec.*	

(continued)

From *Recreation and Parks: The Profession* by Betty van der Smissen, 2005, Champaign, IL: Human Kinetics. Visit www.HumanKinetics.com/RecreationAndParks for a full-color version.

	1886-1900	1901-1910	1911-1920
Recreation (general)	**1892:** Chicago model playgrounds. **1893:** 1st summer playground, Philadelphia. **1893:** MA passed General Enabling Act giving cities right to take land for public playgrounds. **1893:** Boston appointed general superintendent for its 10 summer sand playgrounds. **1899:** NYC opened playgrounds. **1899:** Veblen's *Theory of the Leisure Class* publ.	**1904:** Los Angeles 1st playground board of commissioners. ***1906:*** *Playground Assoc of Am, forerunner NRA, founded.* **1906:** St. John, Canada, est'd its 1st playground. **1907:** Social & civic centers est'd, Rochester, NY. **1907:** 1st Playground Congress held in Chicago; annual congresses held since by NRA/NRPA. **1907:** NJ passed legislation providing for playgrounds & a Playground Board. **1907:** NRA began monthly publ *The Playground*. **1908:** MA playground law required cities of 10,000 population to maintain 1 playground with 1 additional for each 20,000 population.	***1911:*** *PAA became Playground & Rec Assoc of Am.* **1911:** MA extensively broadened playground law & included rec places. **1911:** PA passed laws to create dept of rec in 1st-class cities & to provide for school playgrounds & use of school buildings for rec. **1915:** NJ amended its playground law to Board of Rec Commissioners (general enabling act). **1915:** IA passed Rec Enabling Act for municipalities. **1915-1918:** Neighborhood War Camp Community Service; left buildings to communities. **1916:** NC est'd 1st State Bureau of Community Services. **1916:** Canada, 1st of the community surveys by PRAA developed into annual yearbook. **1917:** Local community centers est'd, Jasper Place Community League & Community Leagues of Edmonton, AB. **1920:** PRAA est'd the Bureau of Colored Workers.
Schools	**1890:** Student unions began. **1896:** J. Dewey's lab school, Chicago. **1898:** Evening rec in NY schools.	**1907:** Social & civic centers opened in Rochester, NY, schools. **1908:** School centers, Gary, IN. **1909:** *Normal Course of Play* publ by PAA.	**1911:** NEA endorsed school ground use for recreation. **1911:** WI mill tax for recreation. **1913:** U of MI & OH State U, 1st to appoint intramural directors. ***1914:*** *Natl Assoc of Student Unions (NASU) est'd.* **1918:** Cardinal principles of secondary education issued by NEA. **1918:** About 50 teachers colleges offered rec centers.
Organized sport (athletics)	**1888:** AAU est'd. **1891:** Naismith invented basketball, Springfield, MA, YMCA. **1895:** Am Bowling Congress. **1895:** Volleyball invented by William Morgan at Holyoke, MA, YMCA. **1896:** 1st modern Olympic games held in Athens.	**1903:** Public school athletic league, NYC. **1903:** 1st professional hockey team. **1903:** Baseball World Series est'd. **1905:** Professional wrestling strong. **1910:** Natl Intercollegiate Athletic Assoc.	**1917:** Natl Commission on Women's Athletics organized.
Religious	**1893:** Intl Walther League (Lutheran) est'd. **1893:** 1st church gym opened (Mormon).		
Nonprofit sector	**1889:** Hull House est'd in Chicago.	**1901:** National Federation of Settlement Houses & Neighborhood Centers est'd. **1902:** Woodcraft Indians founded by E.T. Seton. **1906:** Natl Boys' Clubs est'd. **1908:** Scouts Canada founded. **1910:** Camp Fire Girls, Boy Scouts of Am, 4-H Clubs founded.	**1911:** Natl Conf of Social Centers held in WI. **1912:** Girl Scouts founded. **1912:** U.S. Children's Bureau survey of rec opportunities. **1913:** CFG Bluebird program founded. **1914:** Smith-Lever Act est'd Cooperative Extensive Service & 4-H. **1917:** Commission on Training Camp Activities est'd to coordinate work of voluntary agencies. **1918:** Community Chests & Councils of Am founded as Natl Community Center Assoc.
Therapeutic (recreation/ special population)	**1889:** Boston Normal School of Gymnastics founded to train teachers in Swedish gymnastics; later became Wellesley College's Dept of Health & PE, & remained a center for teacher training in med gymnastics, which evolved into correctives. **1889:** Dudley Allen Sargent, MD, teacher training reqd work in phys diagnosis, methods of prescribing exercise for individuals, phys exercise for treatment of spinal curvature. **1900:** Day school programs for exceptional children.	***1905:*** *Therapeutic Sec of Am PE Assoc formed.* **1908:** Dudley Allen Sargent, MD, emphasized that all PE teachers in the public schools should have training in remedial & corrective gymnastics, physical diagnosis, & massage.	**1918:** WWI increased awareness of disability; people serving in armed forces medical branches est'd private PT practice or taught in corrective physical education. **1919:** National Society for Crippled Children & Adults founded. **1920:** Special attention to children with physical disabilities.

GROUP A: Recreation *(continued)*

From *Recreation and Parks: The Profession* by Betty van der Smissen, 2005, Champaign, IL: Human Kinetics. Visit www.HumanKinetics.com/RecreationAndParks for a full-color version.

1921-1930	1931-1940	1941-1950
1910-1937: Natl Rec Assoc, Joseph Lee, president; Howard Braucher executive director 1909-1949. **1920s:** Phys fitness movement. **1926:** Natl Rec School est'd by PRAA. **1928:** PRAA employed women field workers to focus on public athletics & rec for women. *1930: PRAA became Natl Rec Assoc; changed name of monthly publication to Recreation.* *1930: Research Quarterly began.*	**1932:** 1st Intnl Rec Congress held, Los Angeles. **1933:** Survey of leisure education, Eugene Lies. *1938: Society of Rec Workers founded.* *1938: Rec added as a division to AAHPER's name.* *1938: Canadian PE Assoc founded.* **1940:** Detroit consolidated parks & rec into single dept.	**1941-1945:** WWII, USO Div of Rec founded. **1943:** Canadian natl phys fitness act implemented (repealed 1954). **1944:** Leisure educ for all, Youth Educ Policies Commission. **1945:** 1st state rec commission, NC. *1945: Parks & Rec Assoc of Canada est'd.* **1946:** Society of Rec Workers changed name to American *Rec Society.* **1947:** VT & CA state commissions est'd. **1948:** Am Rec Society acquired full-time executive director & office in Wash. DC. *1948: CPEA incorporated and changed name to CAHPER.* *1950: Armed Forces Section est'd in ARS.*
1922: NASU became interracial; Canadian universities joined. **1924:** MA legislation authorized schools to provide community rec services. **1925:** School playgrounds, Los Angeles. **1925:** Intramurals started in high schools.	*1933: Canadian PE Assoc (CPEA) founded.* **1934:** British Columbia Ministry of Educ est'd classes for rec & PE. **1935:** One-month training institutes est'd by NRA, replaced graduate-level natl rec school. **1937:** 1st college conf on college curricula for training professionals in rec, U of MN.	**1940-1949:** Colleges offer rec majors. **1947:** AACTE developed schedule for evaluation of professional rec curriculum. **1948:** CPEA changed name to CAHPER, adding health & recreation. *1950: Natl Intramural Assoc (NIA) founded.*
1921: U.S. Figure Skating Assoc founded. **1929:** Pop Warner football est'd.	**1934:** Athletic Institute founded. **1939:** Little League Baseball founded.	**1947:** Brooklyn Dodgers hired Jackie Robinson, 1st black player in major leagues. *1950: NATA founded.*
1924: Church rec survey by Rohrer; *Recreation in Theory & Practice* publ. **1926:** E.O. Harbin, Methodist rec leader. **1930:** Northland Rec Leaders Lab, Camp Ihduhapi.	**1935:** Catholic Commission on Scouting.	**1944:** *The Social Recreation Primer* by Robert Tully publ.
1924: 1st Gra-Y Club. **1925:** Y-Indian guides began in YMCA. **1929:** American Youth Hostels Assoc. **1930:** Cub Scouts began.	*1934: National Assoc of Social Workers.*	**1945:** Girls' Club. **1945:** Natl Social Welfare Assembly organized.
1922: Rec staff in veteran's hospitals. **1922:** Intnl Council for Educ of Exceptional Children formed (renamed Council for Exceptional Children, in 1958). **1925:** Am Speech & Hearing Assoc. **1929:** Dept of Rec, Lincoln State School/Health, PE, Leisure, Youth & Human Services est'd. **1930:** Am Red Cross includes rec services. **1930:** IIZ Red Cross Recreators, Lillian Summer's thesis. **1930:** White House Conf on Child Health & Protection dealt with rec services for those with disabilities.	**1935:** 1st U.S. participation in 4th World Games for the Deaf. **1939:** *Sports for the Handicapped* by George T. Stafford of the U of IL publ; 1st indicator of trend away from corrective exercise & toward sports as appropriate school programming for individuals with disabilities. **1939:** George Stafford publ *Sports for the Handicapped.*	**1941:** Menninger Foundation founded. **1941:** 278 rec staff in military hospitals. **1941:** 1st complete supervised patient program. **1943:** Pres of ACA appointed commissioner on specialized camping service. **1945:** VA Rec Service est'd. **1946:** Wheelchair basketball. **1948:** 1st Stokes–Mandeville Games, England. *1948: Hospital Rec Sec, ARS, founded.* **1950:** 1st Natl Conf on Aging.

(continued)

From *Recreation and Parks: The Profession* by Betty van der Smissen, 2005, Champaign, IL: Human Kinetics. Visit www.HumanKinetics.com/RecreationAndParks for a full-color version.

	1951-1960	1961-1970	1971-1980
Recreation (general)	*1952:* Canadian AHPER incorporated (previously Canadian PE Assoc). **1953:** Fed of Natl Professional Organizations organized. *1956: International Rec Service of NRA founded.* **1955:** U.S. Supreme Court ruled racial segregation in public parks & playgrounds unconstitutional. *1956: IRS became independent assoc.* *1956: Am Park & Rec Society est'd as part of NRPA merger.* **1957:** 1st Int'l Congress in Parks & Rec; Intnl Fed of Park & Rec Admin est'd in London. **1958:** Natl cultural center for the performing arts est'd.	**1963:** Civil Rights Act. **1964:** Natl Rec Foundation est'd (Natl Rec School merged into). *1966: Natl Rec & Parks Assoc created by merging Am Rec Society, Natl Conf State Parks, Am Assoc Zoological Parks & Aquariums, American Institute of Park Executives, & Natl Rec Assoc.* **1965:** *Standards & Evaluative Criteria* for parks and rec agencies publ by NRA. *1965: Armed Forces Rec Society, branch of NRPA formed.* *1969: PRAC name changed to Canadian Parks/Rec Assoc.* **1969:** *Journal of Leisure Research* 1st publ.	**1972:** *A Leisure Study Canada,* 1st natl study on leisure, by Statistics Canada. **1972:** ParticipACTION, natl nonprofit agency created to encourage Canadians to be physically active. *1973: World Leisure & Rec Assoc (IRA changed name).* **1973:** NRPA model registration plan developed. **1975:** Leisure Studies Assoc, Canada, founded. **1975:** Canadian Congress on Leisure Research began. **1976:** *Rec Research Review* 1st publ. **1977:** *Leisure Sciences* 1st publ. **1980:** Am Academy for Park & Rec Admin est'd. **1980:** Academy of Leisure Sciences est'd.
Schools	**1950s:** Resurgence of community education-recreation in schools. *1952: NIA became interracial & name changed to Natl Intramural & Rec Assoc.* **1960:** AAHPER recommended NCATE be accepted as accrediting body for rec as part of overall PE & health accreditation. *1960: NIMRA dropped Rec from name & eliminated women from membership.*	**1962:** U of Alberta began its BA program in Rec Leadership; U of British Columbia offered 4-year degree in PE with specialization in rec. **1962-74:** Academic curriculum accreditation developed. *1964: NASU became Assoc of College Unions-Intnl.* **1965:** Natl Intramural Sports Council organized. **1966:** 1st sport mgmt program U of OH in Athens. *1966: ARS became Society of Park & Rec Educators in NRPA merger.* **1970:** NRPA est'd board of professional educ.	**1971:** NIMA accepted women into membership. **1972:** Title IX of Educ Amendment Act, federal law prohibiting gender discrimination in high school & college sports. **1974:** Natl Center for Community Educ est'd; platform supported community rec through schools; Council on Accreditation est'd; accredits academic curriculum. *1975: NIRA changed name to Natl Intramural Rec Sports Assoc.* *1977: CIRA founded.*
Organized sport (athletics)		**1961:** Fitness & Amateur Sports Act passed in Canada.	**1972:** Women competed in NY marathon. **1974:** Little League allowed girls to play baseball & softball. **1975:** ACSM Exercise Director's certification est'd.
Religious	**1950s:** Outdoor ministries, esp organized camping, developed by local churches; natl organizations had natl committees & provided consultants; natl organizations had rec staff to provide consultation to local churches. **1951:** Catholic Youth Organization founded. **1954:** Fellowship of Christian Athletes founded.		**1970s:** Larger churches built gyms & developed youth sport programs.
Nonprofit sector	**1953:** U.S. Dept of Health, Educ, & Welfare est'd. **1956:** YMCA publ *Program Encyclopedia; The Omnibus of Fun* by Eisenberg publ. **1957:** Council on Youth Fitness est'd.		**1975:** Camp Fire admitted boys, dropped girls from name. *1975: Natl Org for Human Service Educ (NOHSE) founded.* **1980:** HEW changed to Dept of Health & Human Services.
Therapeutic (recreation/ special population)	*1952: Rec Therapist Section (AAHPER) founded.* *1953: Natl Assoc of Rec Therapist (NART) founded.* *1953: NRA rec service for people with disabilities est'd.* *1954: American College of Sports Medicine founded.* **1954:** Council for the Advancement of Hospital Rec formed. *1954: Standards for Psychiatric Hospitals and Clinics publ by APA—described activity therapy & separated occupational therapy & recreation.* **1956:** NY Educ Law Rec for Elderly passed. **1957:** Natl Conf on Rec for Mentally Ill. **1958:** Natl Wheelchair Athletic Assoc. **1958:** Fed govt authorized 1st grants to universities & state educ agencies for training personnel in mental retardation; revitalized special educ as a profession. **1960:** 1st Intnl Games for Disabled (wheelchair only) held in Rome; founding of 1st intnl organization for wheelchair sports in England. **1960:** State mental health plans required.	**1961:** Building accessibility standards est'd. **1961:** Natl Conf on Aging. **1961:** Comeback, Inc est'd. *1966: NTRS formed from merger of Hospital Rec Sec of ARS, Rec Therapist Sec of AAHPER, NART, & NRA Rec Services for Handicapped.* **1967:** 1st fed legislation (PL 90-170) enacted; authorized funding specifically for personnel training & research in PE & rec for individuals with disabilities. **1967:** 1st Special Olympics, Chicago. **1967:** National Society for Crippled Children changes name to Easter Seals. **1968:** Architectural Barriers Act passed. **1968:** Special Olympics organization founded. **1969:** 1st fed funds received to support university graduate programs in PE & rec for people with disabilities. **1969:** NTRS convened 1st registration board.	*1971: Recreation: A Medical Viewpoint by Hahn publ.* *1973: Intnl Fed of Adapted Phys Activity founded in Quebec City, ON, by Clermont Simard & colleague.* **1973:** Rehab Act of 1973 passed. **1974:** Educ for All Handicapped Act passed. **1974:** ACA adopted standards for people with phys disabilities. **1974:** The Status of Rec Services for the Handicapped, national Canadian study. **1974:** BEH grant given for rec. *1974: Leisurability periodical started.* **1975:** Ad hoc committee became the Natl Consortium on PE & Rec for the Handicapped (1992 name changed to Natl Consortium for PE & Rec for Individuals with Disabilities). **1976:** The Olympiad for Physically Handicapped held in Canada after Olympics; athletes with amputations & blindness competed for 1st time, marking beginning of modern Paralympics & need for sports knowledge on these conditions. *1977: Dictionary of Occupational Titles included recreational therapist.* **1978:** The Amateur Sports Act (PL-95-606) recognized disability sport organizations & events as part of the U.S. Olympic Committee structure. **1978:** NTRS Board of Registration recognized by NRPA. **1979:** U.S. Olympic Committee organized Committee for Handicapped Sports, now Committee on Sports for the Disabled. **1980:** ACA adopted standards for mentally retarded.

GROUP A: Recreation (continued)

From *Recreation and Parks: The Profession* by Betty van der Smissen, 2005, Champaign, IL: Human Kinetics. Visit www.HumanKinetics.com/RecreationAndParks for a full-color version.

1981-1990	1991-2005
1981: *Canadian Assoc for Leisure Studies est'd.* **1981:** Certified Leisure Professional (CLP) initiated. **1982:** *Leisure Studies* 1st publ. **1983:** Journal of Park & Rec Admin 1st publ. **1985:** *North Am Society for Sport Management est'd.* **1989:** Natl Committee on Park & Rec Agency Accreditation formed.	**1993:** Commission for Park & Rec Accreditation est'd & 1st agencies accredited. **1997:** *Am Leisure Academy est'd.* **1999:** Military version of CAPRA standards adopted. **2000:** North Am Society of HPERD Professionals est'd. **2000:** *WLRA changed name to World Leisure Assoc.* **2005:** *AALR and AAALF (AAHPERD) merged to form Am Assoc for Phys Activity and Rec.*
1983: A study, *Curriculum Guidelines for Canadian Colleges & Universities,* publ by Canadian Parks & Rec Assoc. **1985:** *No Am Society for Sport Mgmt founded.* **1986:** COPA recognition of academic curriculum accreditation.	**2003:** *CIRA merged into CAHPERD.*
1981: Canada Fitness Survey, comprehensive survey completed. **1981:** *IHSA formed.* **1985:** Canadian Fitness & Lifestyle Research Institute created.	**1991:** *Natl Court Club Assoc & Natl Tennis Assoc merged with IHSA to form IHRSA.* **1999:** *Coalition for Active Lifestyles (Canadian) est'd.*
	1990s: Wellness & fitness programs for all ages developed, especially by larger churches; youth adventure/challenge activities & trips began. **1992:** Church Sports Intnl organized. **1996:** God's Great Outdoors radio program launched. **1999:** Assoc of Church Sports & Rec Ministers founded.
1983: *Society for Non-Profit Organizations founded.* **1990:** Boys & Girls Clubs of Am merged.	
1981: Canadian Fed of Sports for the Disabled est'd. **1981:** *NAAP founded.* **1981:** Natl Council for Therapeutic Rec Certification became independent council. **1981:** Declared "Intnl Year of Disabled" by United Nations; began "Intnl Decade of Disabled." **1981:** *Intnl Racquet & Sports Assoc est'd.* **1982:** ACA adopted standards for people with disabilities. **1984:** *Am Therapeutic Rec Assoc founded.* **1984:** Adapted Physical Activity Quarterly & Palaestra began publication. **1986:** Certified Activity Professional est'd by NAAP. **1986:** Historic Strategies for Change in Adaptive PE Conference held in Jasper, Canada; most important date in Canadian APA history. **1988:** 1st unified Paralympics held in Korea; 1st time Paralympics held in same facilities as Olympics. **1990:** American with Disabilities Act (IDEA) enacted. **1990:** Individuals with Disabilities Education Act passed (PL 101-476). **1990:** Active Living Alliance: For Canadians With Disabilities (physical activity focus).	**1992:** Paralympics held in Barcelona; afterward Intnl Paralympic Committee became governing body for Paralympic movement. **1994:** *North Am Fed of Adapted Phys Activity founded.* **1996:** *Canadian Therapeutic Rec Assoc incorporated.* **1996:** Joint task force on credentialing formed by NTRS & ATRA.

From *Recreation and Parks: The Profession* by Betty van der Smissen, 2005, Champaign, IL: Human Kinetics. Visit www.HumanKinetics.com/RecreationAndParks for a full-color version.

29

	1500-1600	1601-1700	1701-1800
GROUP B: Outdoor programming — Organized camping, environmental education, adventure/ challenge			**1749:** Ben Franklin stressed nature & gardening in education. **1799:** 1st church camp revival meetings.
Interpretive services			**1784:** 1st natural history museum to utilize interpretive techniques opened in Philadelphia.
GROUP C: Parks/natural resources — Local parks	**1565:** 1st park land est'd in U.S., Spanish Plaza, St. Augustine. **1583:** Small area of land near St. John's Harbor, Canada, used as public rec space.	**1634:** 1st city park, Boston Commons, est'd. **1641:** Great Ponds Act; fishing & bowling popular activities in MA. **1683:** Wm. Penn plan for Philadelphia contained elements for public parks.	**1733:** James Oglethorpe plans Savannah Public Gardens. **1763:** Halifax Common (Canada) est'd for recreational purposes (skating, lawn tennis, croquet, archery), & to protect open space under mgmt of local horticulture society. **1785:** Battery Park, 1st park proposed in NYC (built in 1826). **1791:** Local park est'd in Wash. DC.
State & provincial parks			
National parks & federal agencies			**1775:** U.S. Army Corps of Engineers est'd (given corp status 1802) **1776-1783:** Natl Military Park System developed to protect 11 natl military sites & 9 battlefields.

From *Recreation and Parks: The Profession* by Betty van der Smissen, 2005, Champaign, IL: Human Kinetics. Visit www.HumanKinetics.com/RecreationAndParks for a full-color version.

1801-1850	1851-1875	1876-1885
1825: Camp for boys who attended Round Hill School. **1837:** Thoreau opened school & introduced field trips for nature study.	**1861:** 1st school camp, Gunnery School for Boys, CT. **1866:** 1st church vacation school with outdoor educ, Boston. **1872:** Fresh air school, NYC.	**1876:** Oswego taught outdoor educ; Rothrock est'd camp for "weakly boys," PA. **1880:** 1st church camp, George Hinckley. **1881:** Camp Chocorua, NH, for healthy boys, Ernest Balch. **1884:** Winthrop T. Talbot est'd 1st commercially successful camp. **1885:** Camp Dudley, YMCA oldest continuously operating camp.
1830: *Birds of America* book publ by John J. Audubon & Wm MacGillimay.	**1869:** 1st park interpretive book, *The Yosemite Guidebook* by Whitney. **1870s:** John Muir leads groups on interpretive hikes into Yosemite backcountry. **1872:** 1st labeled nature trail proposed for Central Park, NYC. **1875:** Agassiz founded 1st org for interpretation trails.	**1883:** American Ornithologists Union & Am Society of Naturalists founded. **1883:** Congress appropriated $40,000 to hire 10 assistants to stem environmental abuse in Yellowstone.
1806: Detroit laid out with public spaces & parks. **1811:** Manhattan Island plans included public square & parade grounds. **1832:** Congress reserved land for public spa in Hot Springs, AR. **1839:** Chicago, park at the old Fort Dearborn site. **1850:** Central Park proposed, designed by Frederick Law Olmstead & Calvert Vaux.	**1851:** Toronto City Council est'd Commission on Public Works & Gardens. **1852:** Gore Park in Hamilton, ON, est'd. **1853:** Central Park in NYC acquired. **1857:** Olmstead appointed supt of Central Park in NYC. **1863:** Boston Park built, Golden Gate Park. **1866:** Prospect Park in Brooklyn and Rock Creek Park proposed. **1867:** Toronto acquired property for Toronto Island Park. **1867:** Fairmont Park, Philadelphia est'd. **1869:** Riverside Park, Chicago. **1874:** Paper presented on state govt's duty to preserve parklands. **1875:** Flint, MI, city park est'd.	**1876:** Washington Park, Chicago. **1878:** Lansing, MI, city park est'd. **1882:** Public Parks Act in Manitoba passed, authorizing cities to acquire land for park development. **1883:** Public Parks Act of Ontario passed allowing development of municipal public parks. **1885:** Central Park, NYC, construction approved by city & state govts. **1885:** Legislation for municipal park systems passed in NJ.
1851: 1st park act passed in NY.	**1864:** Yosemite Valley Park, CA, reserved as a state park, John Muir.	**1885:** NY, in cooperation with Ontario, created Niagara Reservation; Ft. Mackinac, MI, State Reservation Act.
1812: General Land office est'd. **1849:** U.S. Dept of Interior was est'd.	**1862:** U.S, Dept of Agriculture est'd. **1864:** Morrill Land Grant Act (land-grant colleges). **1871:** U.S. Fish Commission created. **1872:** Yellowstone Natl Park est'd. **1875:** Mackinac Natl Park designated; later transferred to state of MI.	**1879:** U.S. Geological Survey est'd. **1885:** Inception of Canadian Natl Park system.

(continued)

From *Recreation and Parks: The Profession* by Betty van der Smissen, 2005, Champaign, IL: Human Kinetics. Visit www.HumanKinetics.com/RecreationAndParks for a full-color version.

31

		1886-1900	1901-1910	1911-1920
GROUP B: Outdoor programming *(continued)*	**Organized camping, environmental education, adventure/ challenge**	**1887:** Fresh air camps est'd, NYC. **1891:** 1st school flower garden, Roxbury, MA. **1891:** YMCA Camp Stevens, operated by Winnipeg YMCA, est'd, oldest continuously operated camp in Canada. **1892:** Camp Arey, a natural science camp for boys, reserved one month for girls, & by 1902 served girls exclusively. **1895:** Nature study movement began in NY. **1898:** 1st YWCA camp for working girls, Providence, YWCA. **1899:** Emma Haskell took her class of children with disabilities on 2-week outing. **1900:** 1st Boys' Club Camp, Salem, MA.	**1902:** Seton's *Birch-Bark Roll* publ. **1902:** 1st all girl camp (private), Laura Matoon Camp, Kehonka, NH. **1903:** 1st official camp conference in Boston. **1907:** Camp Alford Lake, private camp for girls, founded. *1908: Am Nature Study Society founded.* *1910: Camp Directors' Assoc of Am founded (forerunner ACA).* **1910:** 1st college camps.	**1911:** 1st municipal camp. **1912:** Camp Edith Macy, Girl Scouts of America; Disadvantaged Camp, Dubuque, IA. **1914:** 1st Camp Fire Girls camp. **1914:** Vagabonds 1st family camping. **1914:** 1st permanent church camp, Lake Geneva, WI. **1914:** Conservation educ formally adopted as integral part of Boy Scouting. **1916:** Natl Assoc of Directors of Girls Camps formed. **1916:** Camp Walden, ME, Helen Cohen founded, private camp continually owned & operated by 1 family. **1920:** College camp leadership courses.
	Interpretive services	**1887:** Lower Hot Springs cave, Banff, 1st formal interpretive walks conducted by interpreter in Canadian Natl Park. **1888:** 1st nature guide, Enos Mills, Rocky Mt Natl Park. *1893: Am Society of Naturalists founded.* **1895:** 1st park interpretive museum in Canadian natl parks, Banff.	**1904:** 1st interpretive trail est'd in Yosemite. **1905:** Small museum est'd in Casa Grande Ruins in AZ. **1905:** Visitors conducted through cave system, Nakimu Caves, Glacier National Park, BC. *1908: Am Nature Study Society organized.*	**1913:** MI Bureau of History created. **1914:** 1st Canadian Natl Park interpretive publications appeared in Banff. **1918:** 1st U.S. park museum in Mesa Verde, CO. **1919:** Several miles of labeled trails in NY. **1920:** Yellowstone Park museum started. **1920:** Benj. Hyde began outdoor nature museum. **1920:** Ranger & naturalist program at Yosemite. **1920:** 1st U.S. Park Service interpretive programs with govt-employed interpreters in Yosemite & Yellowstone.
GROUP C: Parks/natural resources *(continued)*	**Local parks**	**1890:** Rock Creek Park, Wash., DC est'd by Congress; Charles Eliot citywide park system, Boston. **1892:** Boston Metro System est'd. **1893:** Kansas City, lst park commission. **1895:** Essex Co., NJ, 1st county park legislation. **1898:** Wash., DC acquired 301 park reservations. *1898: New England Assoc of Park Superintendents formed (forerunner AIPE).*	**1903-1904:** Grand Rapids, MI park. *1904: Am Assoc of Park Superintendents (New England Assoc name change).* **1905-1912:** Chicago South Parks (small parks) est'd ($5 million bond issue approved 1903).	**1917:** NJ passed enabling act. **1917:** *Parks* magazine publ quarterly by AIPE.
	State & provincial parks	**1888:** NY appropriated $1 million for land acquisition. **1895:** Mackinac became 1st MI state park.	**1909:** IL 1st state to establish state park system.	**1919:** Indiana 2nd state to establish state park system.
	National parks & federal agencies	**1887:** Rocky Mt Park, Banff, Canada's 1st natl park, est'd. **1888:** Glacier & Yoho Park Reserve, Canada, created. **1891:** Yosemite est'd as natl park. **1895:** Waterton Lakes Forest Park (Canada) est'd. **1899:** Mt Rainer Natl Park created.	**1901:** John Muir authored *Our National Parks*. **1902:** Bureau of Land Reclamation created. **1905:** Bureau of Biological Survey (became U.S. Fish & Wildlife Service). **1906:** Antiquities Act; Devil's Tower Natl Monument, WY. **1908:** Grand Canyon of CO made natl monument. **1909:** 1st complete inventory of water, forest, land, & mineral resources.	**1911:** Dominion Parks Branch, world's 1st natl park service, Canada; Dominion Forest Reserve Act passed. **1915:** Rocky Mt Natl Park est'd. **1915:** Summer hours permitted in natl forests. **1916:** Natl Park Service est'd, Stephen T. Mather 1st director. **1918:** Nationwide survey of rec in natl forests. **1919:** Am Parks Assoc founded. *1920: Canadian Natl Parks Assoc formed (forerunner Natl & Provincial Parks Assoc).*

From *Recreation and Parks: The Profession* by Betty van der Smissen, 2005, Champaign, IL: Human Kinetics. Visit www.HumanKinetics.com/RecreationAndParks for a full-color version.

1921-1930	1931-1940	1941-1950
1921: 1st edition of *Camps & Camping* publ. *1924: Camp Directors of Am Assoc, Midwest Camp Directors Assoc, & Assoc of Girls Camp Directors merged into The Camp Directors' Assoc.* **1925:** Clear Creek Camp, city school district, Los Angeles. **1925:** Life Camps, founded by L.B. Sharp, operating today as Trail Blazer Camps. **1926:** *Camp Directors' Bulletin* 1st publ by ACA. **1930:** *Camp Directors' Bulletin* name changed to *Camping Magazine*.	**1931:** 1st office of Natl Camp Directors Assoc. **1934:** 1st youth hostel in U.S. *1935: Camp Directors' Assoc became Am Camping Assoc (name change).* **1938:** NYC schools experimental camp. *1940: Outdoor Edu Assoc founded.* **1940:** L.B. Sharp Camp, NJ; *Marks of Good Camping* publ.	**1943:** Pres of ACA appointed committee on Specialized Camping Service. **1946:** 1st Girl Scout intercultural camp (for Indian & non-Indian girls.) **1946:** Campbell Loughmiller operated camp for orphans & disadvantaged children. **1947:** Conservation Educ Assoc founded. **1948:** 1st camp standards adopted by ACA. *1950: Canadian Camping Assoc formed.*
1921: Park museum opens in Yosemite. **1923:** Am Nature Assoc began publishing Nature Magazine. **1925:** Yosemite School of Field Natural History opened. **1925:** Nature Trail Research Center, NY. **1926:** 1st nature center est'd in Bear Mt Park, NY. **1926:** CA natural guide program in state parks. **1927:** Outdoor Writers Assoc of Am founded. **1927:** Am Museum of NH opened. **1929:** 1st seasonal interpretive programs, Rocky Mt Natl Parks of Canada, J. Hamilton Laing.	**1931:** Grey Owl employed as interpreter by Parks Canada at Riding Mt, MB, Canada. **1935:** Natl Historical Sites Act passed. **1936:** Natl Audubon state adult camps. **1939:** 25 of 77 agencies in 33 states given naturalist leader course. **1940:** Park naturalists set forth professional standards & practices at 2nd naturalists' conf. **1940:** American Assoc of State & Local History founded.	**1941:** Most state park naturalist programs ended (all but Palisades Interstate park & some in CA, IL, IN, MS, & FL). **1941:** *Field Manual for Museums* publ by Natl Park Service. **1944:** Interpretive events conducted in Banff, Canada, wildlife warden Hubert Green.
1921: Am Institute of Park Executives began publishing *Parks.* **1924:** Natl Capital Park & Planning Commission. **1926:** Rec Act makes land available for recreation. **1928:** Lebert Weir's *Parks: A Manual of Municipal and County Parks* publ. **1930:** Parks became monthly magazine of AIPE.	**1939:** Huron-Clinton Metro Authority, MI, est'd. **1940:** Federal Aid Highway Act funded roadside parks.	
1921: National Conference on State Parks organized. **1930:** Land Transfer Act, Canada.		
1923: Natl Parks Assoc of Canada est'd. **1924:** 1st White House natl conference on outdoor rec. **1930:** Natl Parks Act passed by Canadian Parliament.	**1930s:** Natl Park Service developed Rec Demonstration Areas. **1930-1941:** Great Depression, federal govt financed buildings & leadership; CCC, WPA, PEWA, NYA construct outdoor rec facilities & provide public rec leadership. **1933:** TN Valley Authority est'd. **1934:** U.S. Grazing Service est'd. **1936:** Parks, Parkways, & Rec Area Study Act passed. **1936:** Cape Breton Highlands Natl Parks, Canada, created. **1936:** Lake Mead, NV, 1st natl rec area. **1940:** Bureau of Biological Survey & Bureau of Fisheries merged to become U.S. Fish & Wildlife Service.	**1941:** Rec Div in Office of Community War Services of Fed Security Agency created. **1944:** Flood Control Act gave Army Corps of Engineers ability to operate rec facilities. **1945:** Smokey the Bear originated. **1946:** Bureau of Land Mgmt est'd, merging General Land Office & Grazing Service. **1946:** Fed Interagency Committee on Rec est'd (lasted 16 years). **1950:** Territorial Lands Act (Canadian administered federal crown lands).

(continued)

		1951-1960	1961-1970	1971-1980
GROUP B: Outdoor Programming (continued)	**Organized camping, environmental education, adventure/challenge**	*1950s:* Coalition of Christian Camp & Bible Conference leaders formed Christian Camp & Conf Assoc Intnl. **1952:** Natl Catholic Camping Assoc. **1955:** Outdoor educ project initiated (AAHPER). **1955:** Riley memorial camps for people with physical disabilities opened in Indiana. **1956:** ACA day camp standards adopted. **1957:** Campcraft certification, ACA, est'd; now Outdoor Living Skills (OLS). **1957:** 35 states & 300 school districts have school camping.	**1961:** ACA adopted travel & family camp standards. **1962:** Outward Bound schools, U.S., founded. *1963: CCCAI incorporated & changed name to Christian Camping Intnl.* *1965: Council on Outdoor Educ, AAHPER, est'd.* **1965:** ESEA passed. **1965:** Natl Outdoor Leadership School (NOLS) started. **1967:** ESEA amended. **1970:** Environmental Educ Act passed to promote environmental awareness in schools. **1970:** Fed funds to camps for low-income children.	*1971: NAAEE est'd.* **1971:** Project Adventure began. **1972:** ACA standards greatly revised based on research study. **1973:** 1st conf on outdoor pursuits in higher educ. *1977: WEA founded.* *1977: AEE inc.* **1980-83:** Adventure-based counseling curriculum developed.
	Interpretive services	**1954:** Interpretive programs begin in provincial parks of Ontario. **1955:** Workshops on interpretive programs at Bradford Wood, IN. **1956:** 1st visitor centers built in natl parks. **1957:** *Interpreting our Heritage,* by Freeman Tilden, publ. **1958:** 1st coordinated interpretive service est'd in Ottawa for Canada's national park system.	*1961: ASN became Assoc of Interpretive Naturalists.* **1961:** Visitor Information Service in U.S. Forest Service est'd. **1964:** 1st permanent naturalists located in Canadian Rocky Mt natl parks. **1969:** 1st Canadian wildlife interpretation center (Wye Marsh) opens near Midland, ON.	*1973: Interpretation Canada organized.*
GROUP C: Parks/natural resources (continued)	**Local parks**		**1961:** Open Space & Urban Dev Act passed. **1964:** Natl Assoc of County Officials adopted policy on county parks & rec. **1965:** Land & Water Conservation Fund passed. *1966: National Society for Park Resources est'd.* *1966: NCSP merged into NRPA.*	**1978:** Natl Parks & Rec Act passed providing $1.2 billion fed funds for urban & natl parks.
	State & provincial parks	**1956:** NCSP & Natl Park Service began publishing *Park Practice– Trends, Design, & Grist.*	*1966: NSCP merged into NRPA, became branch.*	*1975: NSCP changed branch name to Natl Society for Park Resources.*
	National parks & federal agencies	**1953:** HEW est'd. **1953:** Cape Hatteras, 1st natl seashore. **1956:** Natl Park Service, Mission 66, 10-year improvement program began. *1957: IFPRA founded.* **1958:** BLM adopted Rec Land Mgmt Policy. **1958:** Natl Outdoor Rec Resources Review Commission (ORRRC) est'd. **1959:** St. Lawrence Seaway open.	**1962:** ORRRC Report issued. **1962:** Rec Advisory Council (fed agencies) est'd. **1962:** 1st World Congress on Natl Parks, hosted by Seattle. **1963:** Natl & Provincial Parks Assoc of Canada formed (now Canadian Parks & Wilderness Society). **1963:** Natl Rec areas est'd; Bureau of Outdoor Rec (BOR) created. **1964:** 1st Canadian comprehensive statement of natl parks policy. **1964:** Water Resources Research Act, Public Land Law Review Committee est'd. **1966:** President's Council on Rec & Natural Beauty. **1967:** Canada initiated the Canadian Outdoor Rec Demand Study (CORDS). *1968: Am Park Assoc changed name to Natl Park & Conservation Assoc.* **1968:** Study of nation's estuaries. **1969:** Natl Environmental Policy Act. **1969:** Council & Citizen's Advisory Committee on Environmental Quality.	**1971:** 1st Canadian Natl Park System Plan approved. *1973: A Legacy for America: 2nd Nationwide Outdoor Rec Plan publ.* **1976:** 1st Northern Natl Park Reserves est'd in Canada. **1976:** Fed Land Policy & Mgmt Act. **1978:** Heritage Conservation & Rec Service created, abolishing BOR. **1979:** Canada revised Natl Parks Policy Service, making ecological integrity a priority. **1979:** Third nationwide outdoor recreation plan released.

From *Recreation and Parks: The Profession* by Betty van der Smissen, 2005, Champaign, IL: Human Kinetics. Visit www.HumanKinetics.com/RecreationAndParks for a full-color version.

1981-1990	1991-2005
1983: *NAEE changed name to North Am Assoc for Environmental Educ.* **1983:** 1st Intnl Camping Congress in Toronto. **1984:** ACA consolidated standards. **1987:** *Coalition for Educ in the Outdoors est'd.* **1988:** Ropes Course Builders' Symposium. **1990:** *Conservation Educ Assoc merged into NAAEE.*	**1992:** 1st CEO Research Symposium. **1993:** *ACCT officially organized.* **1993:** ACA adopted standards for conf & retreat centers. **1993:** *Assoc of Outdoor Rec & Educ est'd.* **1996:** *ACA's private camps incorporated as Assoc of Independent Camps & became ACA affiliate.* **1996:** AEE council on accreditation of adventure programs est'd. **2003:** *COAER est'd.* **2005:** *CAOER and AAALF COE merged into a council under new Am Assoc for Physical Activity and Recreation.*
1984-88: Govt downsizing resulted in drastic budget cuts for interpretation in Canada's natl parks. **1987:** *Assoc of Nature Center Administrators founded as affiliate of Natl Assoc for Interpretation.* **1988:** *AIN & Western Interpreters Association merged into NAI.*	**1991:** Canadian Environmental Advisory Council advised Parks Canada to dedicate more resources to interpretation & educ programs. **1992:** *VSA incorporated.* **1993:** *ANCA incorporated.* **2000:** Panel on the Ecological Integrity of Canada's Natl Parks recommended that interpretation recommend ecological integrity as its core purpose & that interpretive funding be doubled. **2005:** *CCI/USA changed name to Christian Camp and Conference Association (CCCA).*
1981: 1st nationwide conference of State Comprehensive Outdoor Recreation Plan (SCORP). **1983:** Natl Assoc of State Rec Planners formed. **1984:** *PLEA est'd, for local, state, & natl levels.* **1986:** NRPA/SCHOLE electronic network est'd; NRPA board of trustees formally approved 1989-90.	
1984: Canadian Rocky Mt Parks World Heritage Site est'd. **1985:** National Canadian Assembly on national parks & protected areas formed to mark centennial of Canada's natl parks. **1986:** Natl Marine Conservation Areas, Canada, system plan approved. **1987:** Report of Presidential Commission on Americans Outdoors publ, authorized in 1985. **1987:** Outdoor Rec Coalition of Am (ORCA) est'd. **1988:** Canadian Natl Parks Act amended to designate wilderness areas in parks. **1988:** BLM released *Recreation 2000: A Strategic Plan.* **1990:** Canada's Green Plan to complete natl park system by year 2000 publ.	**1994:** *NASRP broadened scope & changed name to National Association of Rec Resource Planners (NARRP).* **1996:** Omnibus Parks & Public Lands Mgmt Act created 5 new NPS units, including 1st tall grass prairie preserve & 9 technical assistance districts for historical/cultural initiatives. **1999:** Parks Canada became separate operating agency. **2000:** New Canadian Natl Parks Act passed. *(Group C, continued)*

From *Recreation and Parks: The Profession* by Betty van der Smissen, 2005, Champaign, IL: Human Kinetics. Visit www.HumanKinetics.com/RecreationAndParks for a full-color version.

	1500-1600	1601-1700	1701-1800
GROUP C: Parks/natural resources *(continued)* — Natural resources (forestry, conservation, preservation)		**1626:** Plymouth Colony ordinance prohibited cutting timber without permission. **1681:** Wm. Penn decreed that for every 5 acres of land cleared, 1 must be left forested. **1691:** British colonial policy reserved large trees for masts.	**1710:** 1st community forest, 110 acres, Newington, NH.
Sportsmen & outdoor organizations		**1639:** Newport, RI, had closed deer season for 6 months. **1647:** MA Bay Colony ordinance regarding hunting. **1694:** 1st closed deer season in MA.	**1710:** In MA hunting waterfowl from sail or blind boats prohibited. **1739:** MA appoints 1st American game–deer warden. **1745:** MD forms club for loading horsemen. **1750:** Sunday hunting permitted. **1771:** NJ antihunting trespass law. **1776:** U.S. closed deer season. **1788:** NY hounding deer prohibited. **1789:** SC buck law protects bucks in summer. **1790:** N.J. Bacrene planted 1st exotic game in U.S., Hungarian partridge.
GROUP D: Private/commercial & tourism — Private & commercial		**1619:** VA prohibits dice & cards. **1664:** 1st public horse race, Long Island, NY.	**1716:** Theater of Williamsburg. **1722:** Billiards began. **1767:** 1st permanent theater in NY. **1773:** 1st American museum. **1794:** 1st ballet performance. **1795:** 1st golf club, SC.
Tourism			**1794:** 1st Am hotel—City Hotel (NY). **1796:** 1st passports issued in U.S.

From *Recreation and Parks: The Profession* by Betty van der Smissen, 2005, Champaign, IL: Human Kinetics. Visit www.HumanKinetics.com/RecreationAndParks for a full-color version.

1801-1850	1851-1875	1876-1885
1828: 1st experimental mgmt of forests by the federal govt in FL. **1849:** 1st swamp land grant in public domain for reclamation.	**1859:** Laws to stop timber poaching. **1860:** Private forest reserves est'd. **1867:** WI & MI conservation practices study. **1872:** NY halts sale of state forest land. **1873:** 1st forestry course, Yale; AAAS urges Congress to promote timber cultivation & forest preservation. **1874:** 1st forestry course, Cornell. **1875:** Am Forestry Assoc est'd.	**1877:** State forestry in 15 states. **1881:** Div of Forestry, Dept of Agriculture created. **1881:** Park Protection Act for wildlife in natl parks. **1882:** 1st forestry congress. **1885:** Adirondack Forest Preserve founded.
1812: General Land Office est'd by Treasury Dept. **1828:** United Bowmen of Pennsylvania. **1842:** 1st boat races in U.S. in Detroit. **1844:** 1st assoc for protecting game. **1846:** Schuetzen Verein Rifle Club, Philadelphia, PA.	**1863:** 1st ski club in U.S., Marquette, MI. **1864:** George Perkins Marsh publ *Man & Nature*. **1864:** 1st resident hunting licenses, NY. **1871:** Natl Rifle Assoc founded. **1872:** 1st rest day for waterfowl hunting. **1872:** Natl Assoc of Amateur Oarsmen est'd. **1873:** Nuttal Ornithological Club est'd. **1875:** Kentucky Derby inaugural race; *Forest & Stream* publ.	**1876:** Appalachian Mt Club organized. **1876:** *Adventures of Tom Sawyer* publ. **1878:** Boston Bicycle Club. **1878:** IA 1st bag limit on prairie chickens. **1879:** Natl Archery Assoc. **1880:** Natl Bicycle Assoc. **1880:** Am Canoe Assoc. **1884:** *Adventures of Huckleberry Finn* publ.
1826: Lyceum Movement. **1840:** P.T. Barnum circuses. **1842:** NY Philharmonic. **1849:** 1st state fair in U.S., MI.	**1854:** Peacedale Mfg Co, RI, opened library for employees & community. **1863:** Roller skating began. **1872:** P.T. Barnum circus train.	**1882:** 1st private country club near Boston.
Early 1820s: Coney Island, NY, exclusive resort area, Manhattan Beach; appreciable number of tourists visited Niagara Falls. **1841:** Thomas Cook founded world's 1st travel agency; considered Father of Modern Travel Agency Operation.	**1851:** Tourists entered Yellowstone by rail. **1867:** 1st railroad across North Am completed, started era of distance train tourism.	**1876:** Sisters Lake resort: hotel, dance hall, & skating rink. **1880:** 1st hotel at Yellowstone. **1882:** Tourist guide publ, Grand Rapids & Indiana RR. **1883:** 1st group of tourists entered Glacier Bay in AK.

(continued)

From *Recreation and Parks: The Profession* by Betty van der Smissen, 2005, Champaign, IL: Human Kinetics. Visit www.HumanKinetics.com/RecreationAndParks for a full-color version.

		1886-1900	1901-1910	1911-1920
GROUP C: Parks/natural resources *(continued)*	**Natural resources (forestry, conservation, preservation)**	**1887:** *Extermination of the Bison*, by William Temple Hornaday publ. **1888:** MI est'd educ services in forestry. **1890:** Forestry on private lands. **1891:** WI 1st private duck refuge. **1891:** 1st natl forest, Yellowstone Timberland Reserve, now part of Shoshone Natl Forest. **1892:** Sierra Club founded by John Muir. **1895:** Am Scenic & Historical Preservation Society. **1897:** 20 million acres of forest est'd as National Forest by President Cleveland. **1898:** Gifford Pinchot named head of U.S. Div of Forestry. **1899:** 1st forest preservation act. **1900:** Society for Am Foresters founded.	**1901:** Assoc for the Protection of the Adirondacks. **1902:** Pelican Island, 1st natl wildlife refuge. **1905:** Div of Forestry became U.S. Forestry Service. **1905:** Natl Audubon Society founded. **1905:** 1st natl game reservation, OK. **1907:** Air Pollution Control Assoc. **1908:** Natl Conservation Commissioner appointed to inventory resources. **1908:** T. Roosevelt's White House Conf of Governors on conservation. **1909:** National Conservation Assoc, a private group organized to replace Natl Conservation Commission. **1909:** North Am Conservation Conf.	**1911:** Dominion Forest Reserve & Parks Act, Canada. **1912:** Rec used in chief forester's report. **1912:** NY College of Forestry, 1st Am school for park administrators & city foresters. **1915:** Ecological Society of Am. **1916:** Agreement between U.S. & Canada for protection of migratory birds; Migratory Bird Treaty. **1917:** Nature Conservancy. **1918:** Save the Redwoods League. **1919:** Natl Parks & Conservation Assoc. **1919:** Leopold & others talk of necessity to preserve wilderness. **1920:** Natl Assoc of State Foresters. **1920:** 1st forest rec plan. **1920:** San Isabel Natl Forest est'd.
	Sportsmen & outdoor organizations	**1886:** Natl Audubon Society, NY. **1886:** 1st natl trapshooting contest. **1887:** Boone & Crockett Club founded. **1900:** U.S. Revolver Assoc.	**1903:** Am Rowing Assoc. **1903:** *Call of the Wild* publ. **1904:** 1st natl ski jumping championship; U.S. Ski Assoc. founded. **1905:** Natl Audubon Society founded. **1905:** 1st public shooting ground, PA. **1910:** Natl Audubon Junior program started. **1910:** Outing Club formed at Dartmouth.	**1911:** North Am Wildlife Foundation. **1914:** U.S. Power Squadron. **1917:** Interstate Trapshooting Assoc. **1917:** Am Horse Show Assoc. **1920:** Amateur Bicycle Club of Am.
GROUP D: Private/commercial & tourism *(continued)*	**Private & commercial**	**1887:** Warner Brothers Co., Bridgeport, CT, erected clubhouse for employees. **1894:** NYC Insurance Co 1st employee rec assoc.	**1902:** Auto races popular.	**1913:** Ping-Pong craze. **1917:** 1st serviceable snowmobile. *1918: Natl Outdoor Showmen's Assoc (NOSA) founded.* *1920: NOSA became Natl Assoc of Amusement Parks (NAAP).*
	Tourism	**1887:** Grand Hotel on Mackinac Island, MI. **1888:** Glacier Park Lodge & Mt Stephan House hotels, Canada, constructed. **1893:** Chicago World's Fair, where world's first Ferris wheel appeared. **1895:** Detroit Convention & Tourist Bureau.	**1903:** Luna Park, self-contained amusement center, offered 5 & 10 cent rides at Coney Island.	**1914:** 1st commercial use of airplanes called "flying boats" transported tourists between FL & Caribbean resorts. *1914: Intnl Assoc of Convention & Visitor Bureaus (IACVB) founded.* *1918: Intnl Assoc of Amusement Parks & Attractions founded.*

1921-1930	1931-1940	1941-1950
1921: U.S. Forest Service & ON, Canada, govt jointly est'd Quetico-Superior Roadless Area. **1921:** Opening of Appalachian Trail. **1921:** Outdoor rec becomes a major forest use. **1922:** Izaak Walton League founded. **1924:** Four million visitors to natl forests. **1924:** 1st wilderness area, NM. *1924: Am Assoc of Zoological Parks & Aquariums founded as affiliate of AIPE.* **1925:** Defenders of Wildlife founded. **1926:** Am Shore & Beach Preservation Society est'd. **1928:** Water Pollution Control Fed. **1930:** Shipstead-Nolan Act protects rec values, MN.	**1932:** Natl Forestry Plan (Copeland Report). **1932:** 1st game survey & conservation plan, IA. **1933:** Soil Erosion Service est'd. **1934:** Prairie States Forestry Project. **1934:** Quetico-Superior Commission. **1934:** First migratory waterfowl stamp issued. **1934:** Coordination Act, use of impounded water for wildlife purposes. **1935:** Historic Sites Act passed. **1935:** Am Wildlife Inst founded. **1935:** Soil Erosion Act passed. **1935:** Wilderness Society founded. **1937:** Ducks Unlimited founded. **1937:** Pittman-Robertson Act (wildlife restoration) passed. **1938:** Am Assoc of Conservation est'd.	**1944:** Soil Conservation Society of Am founded. **1946:** 3rd Am Forestry Congress. **1946:** Division of Rec in the Society of Am Foresters est'd. **1947:** Conservation Educ Assoc. **1948:** Water Pollution Control Act. **1948:** Motorboats forbidden in Quetico-Superior. **1949:** 1st Sierra Club Biennial Wilderness Conf. **1949:** Natl Trust for Historic Preservation est'd. **1949:** 26 million visits to natl forests. **1950:** Fish Restoration & Mgmt Act passed.
1923: Eastern Bird Banding Assoc. **1923:** Amateur Trapshooting Assoc. **1923:** Adirondack Mt Club. **1924:** Am Motorcycle Assoc. **1924:** Am Snowshoe Assoc. **1925:** Appalachian Trail Conf. **1928:** Outboard Boating Club of Am.	**1932:** Fed of Western Outdoor Clubs. **1933:** Natl Muzzle Loading Rifle Assoc. **1935:** Natl Wildlife Fed. **1938:** Natl Council of Jr. Outdoorsmen. **1938:** Natl Ski Patrol est'd. **1939:** Intnl Game Fish Assoc. **1939:** Natl Field Archery Assoc; Am Waterski Assoc.	**1949:** Aldo Leopold's *A Sand County Almanac* publ.
1920-1930: Wild extravagance, private & commercial rec. *1924: Intnl Assoc of Assembly Managers founded as Auditorium Managers Assoc.* **1929:** Country club membership peak reached. **1929:** Henry Ford Museum. **1930:** Flower garden boom.	**1933:** Miniature golf craze. **1937:** Bingo gains natl acceptance. **1937:** Hot rod groups. **1939:** Little League baseball.	*1941: Natl Industrial Rec Assoc (NIRA) founded.* **1946:** Salesmanship Club. **1950:** 1st adventure playground. **1950s:** Commercial rec curriculum in schools resurgence.
1924: Auditorium Managers Assoc (now IAAM) founded. **1925:** Traverse City, MI, Cherry Festival.	**1934:** Canadian Travel Bureau est'd. **1935:** 1st travel information center in U.S., New Buffalo, MI. **1940:** Domestic Travel Act passed, authorizing NPS to manage & promote domestic travel.	

(continued)

From *Recreation and Parks: The Profession* by Betty van der Smissen, 2005, Champaign, IL: Human Kinetics. Visit www.HumanKinetics.com/RecreationAndParks for a full-color version.

		1951-1960	1961-1970	1971-1980
GROUP C: Parks/natural resources *(continued)*	**Natural resources (forestry, conservation, preservation)**	**1952:** Resources for the Future est'd. **1954:** Natl Watershed Congress held. **1957:** Student Conservation program began (now Student Conservation Assoc). **1957:** Institute of Environmental Science est'd. **1957:** U.S. Forest Service launched Operation Outdoors, 5-year program to restore & improve rec facilities in natl forests. **1959:** Good Outdoor Manners Assoc. **1960:** Multiple Use Sustained Yield Act (natl forests) passed making rec a major objective.	**1962:** White House Conference on Conservation held. **1963:** Conservation Law Society of Am est'd. **1964:** Natl Wilderness Preservation system est'd. **1966:** Natl Historic Preservation Act passed. *1966: AAZPA became branch of NRPA.* **1968:** National Trails Systems Act passed. **1968:** Natl Wild & Scenic Rivers Systems Act passed. **1968:** Biosphere Reserve Program started by UNESCO. **1970:** Environmental Protection Agency (EPA) created.	*1971: AAZPA became independent assoc.* **1971:** Ontario Ministry of Natural Resources started active land purchase of prairie communities. **1972:** Coastal Zone Mgt Act. **1973:** Endangered Species Act passed. **1979:** Archeological Resources Protection Act. **1980:** Alaska National Interest Lands Conservation Act.
	Sportsmen & outdoor organizations	**1951:** Nature Conservatory founded. **1954:** Am White Water Affiliation. **1955:** The Trailsmen est'd. **1958:** U.S. Intnl Sailing Assoc. **1959:** CA Open Space Law. **1959:** Underwater Society of Am. **1959:** Trout Unlimited.	**1962:** U.S. Surfing Assoc. **1962:** Rachel Carson's *Silent Spring* publ. **1963:** Shooters Club of America. **1965:** Am Archery Council.	
GROUP D: Private/commercial & tourism *(continued)*	**Private & commercial**	*1951: Industrial Rec Sec of ARS founded.*		*1972: NAAP became Intnl Assoc of Amusement Parks & Attractions.* **1977:** Natl Assoc of Canoe Liveries founded.
	Tourism	**1955:** Disneyland opened in CA, 1st major theme park. *1956: Intnl Festivals Assoc (IFA) est'd.*	**1961:** U.S. Travel Service est'd in Dept of Commerce to promote foreign tourism in U.S. *1970: TTRA est'd.*	*1971: Intnl Society of Travel & Tourism Educators founded.* *1972: MPI founded.*

From *Recreation and Parks: The Profession* by Betty van der Smissen, 2005, Champaign, IL: Human Kinetics. Visit www.HumanKinetics.com/RecreationAndParks for a full-color version.

1981-1990	1991-2005
	1993: Yellowstone to Yukon initiative started by Wildlands Project, Canadian Parks & Wilderness Society, & others. *1994: AAZPA changed acronym to AZA*
1981: Resort & Commercial Rec Assoc founded. *1981: Int'l Racquet & Sportsclub Assoc formed.* *1982: Natl Employee Services & Rec Assoc (NESRA); name change from NIRA.*	*1991: Natl Court Club & Natl Tennis Assoc merged with IRSA into IHRSA.* *1995: NACL changed name to Professional Paddlesports Assoc.* *2000: NESRA changed name to Employee Services Mgmt Assoc (ESMA).*
1981: RCRA est'd. **1983:** Hector Ceballos-Lascurain, naturalist tour operator in Mexico, coined term ecotourism. **1990:** World Travel & Tourism Council founded.	*1995: Society of Travel & Tourism Educators est'd.* *1995: Commercial Rec & Tourism Sec of the NRPA est'd.* *1997: IFA changed name to Intnl Festivals & Events Assoc.* **Late 1990s:** Ecotourism developed extensively worldwide.

From *Recreation and Parks: The Profession* by Betty van der Smissen, 2005, Champaign, IL: Human Kinetics. Visit www.HumanKinetics.com/RecreationAndParks for a full-color version.

Part III

Professional Organizations

Not only is professional organization one of the marks of a profession, but involvement in an organization is a mark of being a professional. Professional organizations offer much to those just starting in the profession and to the experienced professional (see part I). Many organizations serve the recreation and parks field (see figure 1.2), so how can you learn about the organizations appropriate for your interest and determine which professional organizations you should become involved with? This part of the book helps you learn about some of the professional organizations that are available and some information about each.

Only selected national professional organizations whose primary focus is on some aspect of recreation and parks are included; these are considered the principal organizations for park and recreation professionals. Organizations that are listed here without detailed information include the Web address following the initial listing. You can access a list of updated information for and links to the professional organizations at www.HumanKinetics.com/RecreationAndParks. Professional organizations for those involved in specific sports or activities (golf pros, swimming pool personnel, aerobic instructors) are not included. For a listing of these organizations, see the *National Trade and Professional Associations* by Buck Downs (1989-2001, Columbia Books, Washington, D.C.).

CATEGORIES

The professional organizations are divided into six categories. The first five categories are based on the setting or use of recreation as a modality, similar to the categories in part I. Certifying and accrediting agencies and academies is the sixth category.

- **Recreation.** This section includes the professional organizations that traditionally are considered the principal overall recreation and park organizations. They include, but are not limited to, local public recreation and park organizations. The other sections include organizations with a more narrow focus.

- **Natural resources.** These professional organizations focus on the management of natural resources, including county, state, and federal parks and other outdoor areas, as well as historical and cultural development and preservation.

- **Outdoor programming.** These organizations use the environment to effect change in participants, and include organized camping, adventure and challenge, environmental education, and interpretive services.

- **Commercial recreation and tourism.** Organizations representing two aspects of commercial recreation are described: the private for-profit recreation enterprise and employee recreation in enterprises of all types. Tourism-related professional organizations also are included in this section.

- **Therapeutic recreation, disabilities, and fitness.** Therapeutic recreation, recreation for people with disabilities, and fitness are the focus of the professional organizations in this section.

- **Certifying and accrediting agencies and academies.** This section lists organizations that offer overall professional certification and those that accredit an aspect of the recreation and park field. It also describes the nature of the certification or accreditation. The academies to which one may be elected are included in this section.

More than 60 organizations are described, including selected trade associations, which are considered professional organizations in their respective fields. The specific organizations included in each section are set forth in the introduction to each section (see also figure 1.3).

BASIC INFORMATION

Basic information is provided for each of the organizations:

- **Address.** Includes mailing address, phone and fax numbers, e-mail, and Web site.

- **History.** Provides a brief history using selected dates to indicate the organization's evolution, especially name changes. The founding dates and a few other notable dates are highlighted on the time line in part II so that you may locate the organization within a specific time reference. Many of the Web sites also provide a historical overview of the organization.

- **Mission and goals.** This is the most important information regarding an organization, because it indicates the organization's focus. Each organization may state its mission or goals under different headings, such as vision, mission, goals, objectives, or purpose. Not all organizations will state both a mission and goals and objectives. Whatever terminology the organization uses is what's listed here.

- **Structural organization.** Most professional organizations are structured similarly; members elect officers and a board of directors and often create sections or chapters, whether state-based, regional, or institutional. Only unique structural organization is included in the organizational description. Several organizations have established a foundation as a nonprofit 501c(3) organization to take advantage of tax-deductible donations to help finance research, professional development, and special projects.

- **Services and programs.** Most professional organizations provide similar services, including e-mail bulletins for members only, newsletters, journals, other publications, and often a publications or book center. They also sponsor annual conferences, workshops, and institutes for professional development. Certification programs, employment services, legislative and advocacy programs, and information and consultant services are not common. Other services include links to other resources and financial benefits such as travel discounts, insurance, credit cards, and publication and conference registration discounts. Only unique or special programs and services are indicated in the organizational description.

- **Publications.** Most professional organizations produce several publications. Only the primary journal and unique publications are cited.

- **Professional credentialing.** This aspect includes both certifications and accreditation. Organizations specifically focused on accreditation and professional certification programs are listed in the Certification and Accreditation Agencies and Academies category on page 97. If an organization has developed an extensive code of ethics or published professional practices, this is noted. For details regarding other available certifications, go to the organization's Web site.

If nothing is special or unique about a particular organization for one of these aspects, that aspect has not been included. Go to the organization's Web site for more detailed information. The information provided here is intended to highlight the most useful information for those learning about the profession.

Active professional organizations continually upgrade their membership services. Thus, it is essential to visit an organization's Web site regularly to update your knowledge of its services and activities. Each organization's Web address is listed under its address. You can access a list of updated information for and links to the organizations at www.HumanKinetics.com/RecreationAndParks.

MEMBERSHIP

As a recreation and parks professional you should be an *active* member in at least one of the organizations that serves your area of professional work or interest. But you should also be familiar with *all* the other organizations in that area, perhaps holding a membership to receive publications and other information, even if you are not active. Further, you should check into a related category for additional organization resources. For example, if your interest area is recreation, you should also investigate the related section on therapeutic recreation, disabilities, and fitness for organizations that provide community services for people with disabilities. Or, if your interest is in natural resources, check the outdoor programming category. Placement in one section does not mean an organization does not also contribute to another section; most organizations serve multiple interests.

The benefits of membership are discussed in part I. However, while you may be a member of a national organization, it is very important to learn about and participate in state or regional chapters, sections, or branches (see the organization Web site). Meetings are closer and usually less expensive to attend, making it easier to be an active member. The organization's Web site provides professional news, information of local importance, and a network of nearby professionals. Membership information and applications are usually available on an organization's Web site.

RECREATION

Organizations in this category can be placed in one of three classifications. The first classification is general, and encompasses various facets of recreation. Two general organizations, American Alliance for Health, Physical Education, Recreation and Dance (AAHPERD) and National Recreation and Park Association (NRPA), are umbrella organizations; each is composed of several national associations or branches. The various associations or branches are set forth here in the description of the parent organization in this part, but certain individual associations or branches are described in the category to which each relates most closely.

AAHPERD: American Alliance for Health, Physical Education, Recreation and Dance

AAPAR: American Association for Physical Activity and Recreation

CAHPERD: Canadian Association for Health, Physical Education, Recreation and Dance

NRPA: National Recreation and Park Association

AFRS: Armed Forces Recreation Society

APRS: American Park and Recreation Society

SPRE: Society of Park and Recreation Educators

CPRA: Canadian Parks and Recreation Association

WLA: World Leisure Association

The second classification includes organizations with a specific focus:

NIRSA: National Intramural-Recreational Sports Association

CIRA: Canadian Intramural Recreation Association

NASSM: North American Society for Sport Management

ACUI: Association of College Unions International

The third classification is directed toward human services and the nonprofit sector:

NOHSE: National Organization for Human Service Education

SNPO: Society for Nonprofit Organizations

A few additional professional organizations have been included, but are not described in detail. Review them for possible interest.

CALS: Canadian Association for Leisure Studies (www.eas.ualberta.ca/edj/cals)

CCAA: Canadian Centre for Activity and Aging (www.uwo.ca/actage/centre)

IAKS: International Association for Sports and Leisure Facilities (www.iaks.org/en/en11.htm)

LSA: Leisure Studies Association (www.leisure-studies-association.info/LSAWEB/Index.html)

NCEA: National Community Education Association (www.ncea.com)

NCRA: National Correctional Recreation Association (www.strengthtech.com/correct/ncra)

SRLA: Sport and Recreation Law Association (www.ithaca.edu/srla)

▌*American Alliance for Health, Physical Education, Recreation and Dance (AAHPERD)* ▌

Address

1900 Association Dr.
Reston, VA 20191
phone: 800-213-7193
fax: 703-476-9527
e-mail: varies by specific association, project, or service (see Web site)
www.aahperd.org

History

1885—The association was founded as the American Physical Education Association.

1938—The American Association for Health and Physical Education added Recreation to its title.

1965—The Council on Outdoor Education (COE) was established. One of AAHPERD's pertinent councils; see the section on Outdoor Programming, page 69.

1978—Added Dance to title, and became the American Alliance for Health, Physical Education, Recreation and Dance.

2003—Council for Adventure and Outdoor Education/Recreation (CAOER) established, merging American Association for Leisure and Recreation's (AALR) and American Association for Active Lifestyles and Fitness' (AAALF) outdoor units.

2005—AALR and AAALF merged into a new association (AAPAR) within AAHPERD; see Web site for developments.

Mission and Goals

AAHPERD's mission is to promote and support creative lifestyles through high-quality programs in health, physical education, recreation, dance, and sport, and to provide members with professional development opportunities that increase knowledge, improve skills, and encourage sound professional practices. The purpose of AAHPERD's national associations include the following:

- Develop and disseminate professional guidelines, standards, and ethics
- Enhance professional practice by providing opportunities for professional growth and development
- Advance the body of knowledge in the fields of study and in the professional practice of the fields by initiating, facilitating, and disseminating research
- Facilitate and nurture communication and activities with other associations and other related professional groups
- Serve as their own spokespersons
- Promote public understanding and improve government relations in their fields of study
- Engage in future planning
- Establish and fulfill other purposes that are consistent with the purpose of the alliance

Structural Organization

AAHPERD is an alliance of five national associations:

- AAPAR: American Association for Physical Activity and Recreation, which is composed of the following councils grouped into three divisions:
    - People Division (Adapted and Therapeutic Council; Aging and Adult Development Council; an1d Children, Youth, and Families Council)
    - Programs Division (Adventure and Outdoor Education/Recreation Council; Aquatics Council; Community Recreational Sports Council; and Fitness and Wellness Council)
    - Management Division (Measurement and Assessment Council; Recreation Program and Event Management and Supervision Council; Safety, Security, and Risk Management Council; and Venue Management and Design Council)
- AAHE: American Association for Health Education (serves health educators and other professionals who promote health)
- NAGWS: National Association for Girls and Women in Sport (promotes equity issues in sports, including equal funding, quality, and respect for girls' and women's sport programs)

- NASPE: National Association for Sport and Physical Education (seeks to enhance knowledge and professional practice in sport and physical activity through scientific study and dissemination of research-based and experiential knowledge to members and the public)
- NDA: National Dance Association (seeks to increase knowledge, improve skills, and encourage sound professional practices in dance education through high-quality dance programs)

In addition to these five associations, the Research Consortium provides services and publications that assist the HPERD researchers and promotes the exchange of ideas and scientific knowledge within the HPERD disciplines.

Publications

Journal of Physical Education, Recreation and Dance (JOPERD): Principal journal, published nine times a year.

Research Quarterly for Exercise and Sport: Advanced papers in exercise and sport science; annual supplement of research abstracts.

Professional Credentialing

- NASPE works jointly with the North American Association for Sport Management (NAASM) on sport management university curriculum program standards.
- The National Council for Accreditation of Teacher Education (NCATE) accredits university academic physical education programs, and sometimes recreation is included.
- AALRPAF (formerly AALR), jointly with the National Parks and Recreation Association (NRPA), sponsors the national Council on Accreditation, which accredits university academic recreation and park curricula. (See Certification and Accreditating Agencies and Academics on page 97 for details.)
- AAPAR (formerly AALR) is a member of the Commission for Accreditation of Park and Recreation Agencies (CAPRA). (See Certification and Accreditating Agencies and Academics on page 97 for details.)
- NASPE has developed standards for kindergarten through 12th grade physical education for athletic coaches and for beginning teachers.

| *American Association for Leisure and Recreation (AALR)* |

In 2005, merged with AAALF to become American Association for Physical Activity and Recreation (AAPAR), an association of AAHPERD.

Address

AALR National Office
1900 Association Dr.
Reston, VA 20191
phone: 800-213-7193 x472
fax: 703-476-3472
e-mail: aalr@aahperd.org
www.aahperd.org/aalr

History

1938—The American Association for Health and Physical Education added Recreation as a division and added Recreation to its title to become the American Association for Health, Physical Education, Recreation and Dance.

1974—The Recreation Division became AALR.

2005—AALR and AAALF merged to form a new American Association for Physical Activity and Recreation (AAPAR).

Mission and Goals

AALR's mission is to promote and support education, leisure, and recreation by developing quality programming and professional training; providing leadership opportunities; disseminating quality guidelines and standards; and enhancing public understanding of the importance of leisure and recreation in maintaining a creative and healthy lifestyle.

The organization's goals and objectives include the following:

- Serving as a forum for professionals, students, and organizations to educate and exchange information and ideas on leisure and recreation services
- Developing and promoting professional standards for education, leisure, and recreation services
- Increasing public awareness, understanding, appreciation, and support for lifelong education, leisure, and recreation services
- Encouraging professional training for education, leisure, and recreation services
- Advancing, encouraging, conducting, and publishing scientific knowledge and research in the field of education, leisure, and recreational services

Services and Programs

- Play and playground safety
- Family recreation
- Outdoor adventure, education, and recreation (fishing and boating educational project)
- Kids of Hope
- American Leisure Academy (See the section on Certifying and Accrediting Agencies and Academies, page 97.)

Professional Credentialing

AALR and the NRP jointly sponsor the national Council on Accreditation (COA), which accredits recreation and park university academic programs. AALR is a member of the Commission for Accreditation of Park and Recreation Agencies (CAPRA). See Certifying and Accrediting Agencies and Academies, page 97.

| *Canadian Association for Health, Physical Education, Recreation and Dance (CAHPERD)* |

Address

2197 Riverside Dr., Ste. 403
Ottawa, ON, Canada K1H 7X3

phone: 613-523-1348 or in Canada 800-663-8708
fax: 613-523-1206
e-mail: info@cahperd.ca
www.cahperd.ca

History

1933—Founded as the Canadian Physical Education Association (CPEA).

1948—CPEA incorporated and changed its name to Canadian Association for Health, Physical Education, and Recreation (CAHPER).

1975—The position of vice president for recreation was eliminated, although Recreation remained in the title of the organization.

1994—Dance was added to the name.

2003—Canadian Intramural and Recreation Association (CIRA) merged into CAHPERD.

Mission and Goals

CAHPERD's vision is that all Canadian children and youth live physically active and healthy lives.

CAHPERD's mission is to advocate for and provide education about quality physical and health education within supportive school and community environments. CAHPERD is the national association for physical and health education professionals. It offers leading-edge information, programs, resources, advocacy, and periodicals relevant to anyone who wants children to lead more active, healthy lives, and speaks out on the following:

- The vital role physical and health education play in the development of children
- The personal and societal value of maintaining a healthy mind and healthy body
- The inherent right of all people to equal access and the opportunity to participate in physical activity
- The understanding that health and physical education are the foundations of active, healthy living and quality of life

Services and Programs

CAHPERD focuses on three major program areas:

- Quality daily physical education
- Quality school health
- Intramural recreation, through its program advisory committee

While CAHPERD's recreation activity was muted with the development of the Canadian Parks and Recreation Association, CAHPERD offers a place for individuals interested in intramural and recreation programs within the education community. Physical activity and its role in leisure and initiatives along this line have increased since the turn into the 2000s.

CAHPERD partners with other organizations extensively. It sponsors the Active Healthy School Community initiative. It also serves as secretariat to the Coalition for Active Living and the Sport Matters Group (SMG).

Publications

The Physical and Health Education Journal (PHE Journal): Published quarterly.

Advante: Research periodical published three times a year.

| *National Recreation and Park Association (NRPA)* |

Address

22377 Belmont Ridge Rd.
Ashburn, VA 20148
phone: 800-626-NRPA (6772)
fax: 703-858-0794
e-mail: info@nrpa.org
www.nrpa.org

History

1966—Five organizations merged into the NRPA. (Frequently, 1965 is given as the date of merger. Organizing and filing the incorporation papers took place in 1965; however, the new organization, NRPA, officially began Jan. 1, 1966.)

For a better understanding of the origins of NRPA, a brief history of each of the organizations prior to the merger is given to indicate the evolution of NRPA and what aspects of the field came together.

National Recreation Association (NRA)

1906—Playground Association of America (PAA) founded.

1911—Name changed to Playground and Recreation Association.

1930—Name changed to National Recreation Association. NRA was a voluntary service organization, although recreation and park professionals were active participants.

In the merger, the APRS branch was formed to serve the local recreation and park professionals.

American Institute of Park Executives (AIPE)

1898—New England Association of Park Superintendents founded.

1904—Name changed to American Association of Park Superintendents.

1921—Name changed to American Institute of Park Executives.

In the merger the National Society for Park Resources (NSPR) branch was formed to service the park and natural resource professionals.

American Recreation Society (ARS)

1938—Founded as the Society of Recreation Workers, as an organization specifically for professionals, separate from NRA.

1946—Name changed to American Recreation Society.

The ARS was composed of several sections. In the merger, branches formed to serve particular sections. For example, the hospital section became the National Therapeutic Recreation Society (NTRS), educators formed the Society of Park and Recreation Educators (SPRE), and the armed forces section became the Armed Forces Recreation Society (AFRS). The industrial recreation section did not form a branch and those professionals became part of the National Industrial Recreation Association (NIRA), which declined to be a part of the merger (see listing for Employee Services Management Association, page 84). Several sections, such as the religious section and voluntary agencies section, were not accommodated and these members either joined related branches or left the association.

National Conference of State Parks (NCSP)

1921—Organization founded.

1966—In the merger, became part of the National Society for Park Resources (NSPR) branch; however, a National Conference of State Park Directors was established later, but membership was limited to only the state park directors.

American Association for Zoological Parks and Aquariums (AZA)

1924—Founded as an affiliate of American Institute of Park Executives (AIPE).

1971—In the 1966 merger, as an affiliate of AIPE, was a separate branch, but withdrew shortly after the merger and reestablished itself as a separate national organization.

1994—Changed its acronym to AZA (see the section on Natural Resources, page 64 for more information).

Mission and Goals

NRPA's mission is to advance parks, recreation, and environmental conservation efforts that enhance the quality of life for all people.

NRPA believes that the field of recreation and parks should accomplish the following:

- Enhance the human potential by providing facilities, services, and programs that meet the emotional, social, and physical needs of communities
- Articulate environmental values through ecologically responsible management and environmental education programs
- Promote individual and community wellness that enhances the quality of life for all citizens
- Utilize holistic approaches to promote cultural understanding, economic development, and family and public health and safety by working in coalitions and partnerships with allied organizations
- Facilitate and promote the development of grassroots, self-help initiatives in communities across the country

The organization's goals include the following:

- Promote public awareness and support for recreation, park, and leisure services as they relate to the constructive use of leisure and thereby to the social stability of a community and the physical and mental health of individuals; NRPA strives to promote public awareness of the environmental and natural resource management aspects of recreation and leisure services
- Facilitate the development, maintenance, expansion, and improvement of society and environmentally relevant public policy that supports recreation, parks, and leisure programs and services

- Enhance the development of parks, recreation, and tourism professionals and to provide services that contribute to the development of NRPA members
- Promote the development and dissemination of knowledge in order to improve services, increase understanding of leisure behavior, and expand the body of knowledge relative to recreation and park programs and services

Structural Organization

NRPA's eight branches and two sections address the diverse interests in the recreation and park field. For more information about the other branches and sections, see NRPA's Web site.

- American Park and Recreation Society (APRS). Composed primarily of professionals who work in public agencies to deliver park, recreation, and leisure services. Members represent diversified park or recreation interests in government, private agencies, and commercial organizations.
- Armed Forces Recreation Society (AFRS) is an organization for armed forces Morale, Welfare, and Recreation (MWR) professionals, technicians, and all others who wish to affiliate with its mission and for recreation and park professionals who work in military settings worldwide.
- Citizen-Board Member (C-BM) includes elected and appointed members of local recreation and park boards, including friends groups and citizen advocates.
- Commercial Recreation and Tourism Section (CRTS) supports organizations and individuals working in the commercial sector (see the section on Commercial Recreation and Tourism, page 83).
- Leisure and Aging Section (LAS) serves professionals and citizens interested in leisure and aging issues.
- National Aquatic Branch (NAB) represents recreation and park professionals who work in aquatic settings.
- National Society for Park Resources (NSPR) includes recreation and park professionals who work in natural resources, parks, and conservation areas (see the section on Natural Resources, page 64).
- National Therapeutic Recreation Society (NTRS) serves recreation and park professionals, organizations, and students interested in therapeutic recreation services (see the section on Therapeutic Recreation, Disabilities, and Fitness, page 90).
- Society of Park and Recreation Educators (SPRE) serves educators in parks, recreation, leisure, and tourism.
- Student Branch (SB) serves students interested in becoming parks, recreation, and tourism professionals.

NRPA has three national affiliates:

- Ethnic Minority Society (EMS). See the NRPA Web site.
- Park Law Enforcement Association (PLEA). See the section on Natural Resources, page 64.
- National Association of County Park and Recreation Officials (NACPRO). See the section on Natural Resources, page 64.

Publications

Parks & Recreation: Principal monthly magazine.

Journal of Leisure Research: Published quarterly.

Professional Credentialing

- National Certification Board administers the Certified Park and Recreation Professional (CPRP) program.
- NRPA certifies therapeutic recreation professionals and participates in National Council for Therapeutic Recreation Certification (NCTRC), the primary therapeutic recreation certification body (see the section on Certifying and Accrediting Agencies and Academies, page 97).
- NRPA accredits academic programs and, with AALR, jointly sponsors the Council on Accreditation (COA).
- The Commission for Accreditation of Park and Recreation Agencies (CAPRA) accredits recreation and park agencies; this program is jointly sponsored with the American Academy for Park and Recreation Administration (AAPRA).

▌ *Armed Forces Recreation Society (AFRS)* ▌

A branch of NRPA

Address

22377 Belmont Ridge Rd.
Ashburn, VA 20148
phone: 703-858-2199
fax: 703-858-0707
e-mail: info@nrpa.org
www.nrpa.org (select Branches, then select AFRS)

History

1950—Originally was armed forces section (AFS) of the American Recreation Society.

1966—In merger AFS became a branch of NRPA called Armed Forces Recreation Society (AFRS).

Mission and Goals

AFRS is dedicated to being the leading force in morale, welfare, and recreation by contributing to readiness and combat capability through quality of life and sense of community; by providing the membership a common forum to promote communication, networking, professional and staff development, and recognition of professional achievement at the national level.

The organization's goals include the following:

- Maintain and expand a society of dedicated individuals who plan, design, manage, and deliver quality recreational opportunities for authorized users of Morale, Welfare, and Recreation
- Provide opportunities for members of the society to enhance professional and personal skills
- Encourage individuals to obtain and maintain an appropriate level of professional certification
- Forge and strengthen partnerships with other elements within NRPA and other relevant organizations
- Encourage development and dissemination of current information on issues and topics relevant to the mission and roles of armed forces recreational personnel

- Market and promote the values and benefits of armed forces recreation as a contributing factor in providing recruitment, readiness, retention, and quality of life
- Recognize individuals and installations for outstanding contributions to armed forces recreation or to the Armed Forces Recreation Society
- Advocate for progressive national polices that support recreation for the armed forces

Professional Credentialing

AFRS has a member on the Commission for Accreditation of Park and Recreation Agencies (CAPRA), which has an accreditation program for military installations. (See the section on Certifying and Accrediting Agencies and Academies, page 97)

| *American Park and Recreation Society (APRS)* |

A branch of NRPA

Address

22377 Belmont Ridge Rd.
Ashburn, VA 20148
phone: 703-858-0784
fax: 703-729-0794
e-mail: aprs@npra.org
www.nrpa.org (select Branches, the select APRS)

History

1965—Established as a branch in the NRPA merger. It is the largest professional branch of NRPA.

Mission and Goals

The organization's mission is to strengthen the recreation and park profession and to enhance a community's quality of life.

The organization's purposes include the following:

- Being an advocate for recreation and park in the United States and Canada
- Fostering professional growth and development of recreation and park personnel, thus improving the delivery of leisure services
- Providing advice to NRPA in achieving overall organizational goals
- Gathering and disseminating information on significant recreation and park issues

Professional Credentialing

No separate credentialing services exist. Members participate in NRPA's Certified Park and Recreation Professional (CPRP) certification program and the CAPRA accreditation program. (See the section on Certifying and Accrediting Agencies and Academies, page 97.)

❚ *Society of Park and Recreation Educators (SPRE)* ❚

A branch of NRPA

Address

22377 Belmont Ridge Rd.
Ashburn, VA 20148
phone: 703-858-2150
fax: 703-858-0794
e-mail: info@nrpa.org
www.nrpa.org (select Branches, then select SPRE)

History

1938—Established as the Society of Recreation Workers, an organization for professional personnel, separate from NRA.

1946—Name changed to American Recreation Society; a professional educators' section formed.

1966—With NRPA merger, SPRE branch was established to serve professionals in educational settings.

Mission and Goals

SPRE is committed to providing a forum for interaction among recreation and park scholars and for disseminating information about matters related to educational issues in the parks, recreation, and leisure field.

The organization's goals and objectives include the following:

- Serve as a forum for identification, analysis, and solution of issues affecting the community of scholars in all areas of recreation and parks
- Stimulate quality research efforts and facilitate distribution of research findings through publications, symposia, and workshops
- Strengthen the link between recreation and park practitioners and educators for the overall advancement of the field

Publications

Schole: A Journal of Leisure Studies and Recreation Education: Published annually.

Journal of Leisure Research.

Curriculum Catalog: Published biannually, includes information about colleges and universities offering major curricula in recreation and park.

Professional Credentialing

No credentialing services exist; however, academic programs are accredited by the national Council on Accreditation. (See the section on Certifying and Accrediting Agencies and Academies, page 97.)

| *Canadian Parks and Recreation Association (CPRA)* |

Address

2197 Riverside Dr., Ste. 404
Ottawa, ON, Canada K1H 7X3
phone: 613-523-5315
fax: 613-523-1182
e-mail: cpra@cpra.ca
www.cpra.ca

History

1945—Founded as Parks and Recreation Association of Canada (PRAC).

1969—Name changed to Canadian Parks/Recreation Association (CP/RA); slash dropped later and replaced with "and."

Mission and Goals

CPRA's vision is to serve as the national voice for a vibrant grassroots network with partnerships that connect people who build healthy, active communities and affect the everyday lives of Canadians.

CPRA exists to build healthy communities and enhance the quality of life and environments for all Canadians through collaboration with its members and partners.

To this end, the association will do the following:

- Be a national voice for recreation and park
- Build and nurture partnerships
- Advocate recreation and park as essential to individual, family, and community health and well-being
- Communicate and promote the values and benefits of recreation and park
- Respond to the diverse and changing needs of members
- Provide educational opportunities

Publications

Parks and Recreation Canada: Since 2003 the magazine has temporarily suspended publication while the information and communication needs are being evaluated during the association's strategic planning process.

| *World Leisure Association (WLA)* |

Address

World Leisure Secretariat
203 Wellness/Recreation Center
University of Northern Iowa
Cedar Falls, IA 50614-0241
phone: 319-273-6279
fax: 319-273-5958
e-mail: secretariat@worldleisure.org
www.worldleisure.org

History

See *WLRA Journal,* vol. 23, 1981, 25th Anniversary Issue for the history of first 25 years.

1953—International Recreation Service of NRA established after a tour of 13 countries in 1952 by Tom Rivers, assistant executive director of NRA.

1956—International Recreation Association founded as independent association.

1973—Name changed to the World Leisure and Recreation Association.

2000—Name changed to World Leisure Association.

Mission and Goals

The World Leisure Association promotes leisure as integral to social, cultural, and economic development through the following:

- Social development: enlarging people's choices
- Cultural development: affirming and enriching cultural identities
- Economic development: achieving sustainable and well-distributed growth

More specifically, World Leisure pursues these goals by doing the following:

- Fostering research and inquiry
- Advocating the importance of leisure
- Directing programming at policy and executive development

Each commission and working group has its own goals and objectives, projects, and programs (see WLA's Web site).

Structural Organization

World Leisure is composed of eight commissions, two working groups, and three regional organizations. First a group of members interested in either tourism or children and youth form a working group, then after the group has met certain criteria it may be designated a commission. The commissions are as follows:

- Commission on Volunteerism
- Commission on Leisure and Later Life
- Commission on Law and Policy
- Commission on Access and Inclusion
- Commission on Research (jointly sponsored with CBA International Leisure Recreation Tourism Abstracts)
- Commission on Leisure Education
- Commission on Women and Gender
- Commission on Leisure Management

The three regional organizations within WLA are as follows:

ALATIR: Association Latino-Americana de Tiempo Libre & Recreation

ANZALS: Australian and New Zealand Association for Leisure Studies

ELRA: European Leisure and Recreation Association

Many parks and recreation associations exist throughout the world that are not a part of WLA. See www.world-playground.com for some of these associations.

Services and Programs

- World Leisure Centre of Excellence (WICE) is an educational program in collaboration with Wageningen University and Research Center in the Netherlands; offers a master of science degree in leisure, tourism, and environments.
- The organization developed a Charter for Leisure in1970 and revised it in 1979. It was approved by the board of directors in 2000.
- The International Charter for Leisure Education was created in 1993.
- The International Position Statement on Leisure Education and Community Development was developed in 1998.

Publications

World Leisure Journal: Published quarterly.

National Intramural-Recreational Sports Association (NIRSA)

Address

NIRSA National Center
4185 SW Research Way
Corvallis, OR 97333-1067
phone: 541-766-8211
fax: 541-766-8284
e-mail: nirsa@nirsa.org
www.nirsa.org

History

1950—Founded as the National Intramural Association (NIA) at Dillard University, New Orleans, by 11 black colleges.

1952—NIA became interracial and name changed to National Intramural and Recreation Association (NIRA).

1960—Dropped Recreation from name and eliminated women from membership (women had been permitted to attend annual conferences from 1954 to 1959).

1971—Constitution was amended to accept women into membership.

1975—Name was changed to the National Intramural-Recreational Sports Association.

Mission and Goals

The organization's mission is to provide for the education and development of professional and student members and to foster quality recreational programs, facilities, and services for diverse populations. NIRSA demonstrates its commitment to excellence by utilizing resources that promote ethical and healthy lifestyle choices.

Structural Organization

To facilitate the association's mission, three independent legal entities have been formed: NIRSA, The NIRSA Foundation (established 1992), and NIRSA Services Corporation (established 1999).

Services and Programs

- The National School of Recreational Sports Management offers programs on two levels: one for new professionals or those with one to five years of experience and one for professionals with five or more years of experience. The first school was held in 1989.
- The National Executive Development Institute is for upper-level administrators; first institute was held in 1990.

Publications

Recreational Sports Journal (RSJ): First published in 1977.

NIRSA Journal: Published twice a year; official publication of the NIRSA Foundation, research based.

Professional Credentialing

Certified Recreational Sports Specialist (CRSS) was instituted in 1981. A code of ethics for professional members and for student members was adopted in 1984.

Canadian Intramural Recreation Association (CIRA)

In April, 2003, CIRA (founded in 1977) transferred its programs and resources to the Canadian Association for Health, Physical Education, Recreation and Dance (CAHPERD), which established the Intramural Recreation Program Advisory Committee. Intramural recreation joins quality daily physical education and quality school health as one of CAHPERD's three major program areas. See the listing for CAHPERD, page 50, for contact and other information.

North American Society for Sport Management (NASSM)

Address

c/o Kinesiology Department
University of New Brunswick
Fredericton, NB, Canada E3B 5A3
phone: 506-453-666
fax: 506-453-3511
e-mail: NASSM@unb.ca
www.unb.ca/sportmanagement/nassm.htm

History

1985—Founded by a group of sport management academicians in order to identify common needs and concerns within the sport management industry.

1989—NASSM joined National Association for Sport and Physical Education (NASPE) on a task force to develop curricular guidelines for a sport management major.

Mission and Goals

The organization's purpose is to promote, stimulate, and encourage study, research, scholarly writing, and professional development in the area of sport management—both theoretical and applied aspects.

Publications

Journal of Sport Management.

Professional Credentialing

NASSM, jointly with NASPE (an association of AAHPERD), established Sport Management Program Standards and Review, an academic curriculum approval process, in 1993. The Sport Management Program Review Council (SMPRC) administers the program.

| *Association of College Unions International (ACUI)* |

Address

ACUI Central Office
One City Centre, Ste. 200
120 W. Seventh St.
Bloomington, IN 47404-3925
phone: 812-855-8550
fax: 812-855-0162
acui@indiana.edu
www.acui.org

History

1914—Founded as National Association of Student Unions. The association evolved under various names: American Association of Student Unions, Association of College and University Unions, and Association of College Unions.

1922—Became international when Canadian universities joined.

1964—The association became Association of College Unions-International (ACU-I); the hyphen was deleted in 1996.

Mission and Goals

The ACUI supports its members in developing a sense of community through education, advocacy, and the delivery of service. Its core purpose is to be the leader in advancing campus community builders.

Structural Organization

The organization is composed of four education councils:

- Administration, Finance, and Management
- Auxiliary Services
- Campus Life and Program Management
- Facilities and Operations

Publications

The Bulletin: Magazine published bimonthly.

▌ *National Organization for Human Services Education (NOHSE)* ▐

Address

5601 Brodie Lane, Ste. 620-215
Austin, TX 78745
phone: 512-692-9361
fax: 512-692-9445
e-mail: info@nohse.org
www.nohse.com

History

1975—Organization established.

Mission and Goals

The purpose of NOHSE is to accomplish the following:

- Provide a medium for cooperation among human service organizations and individual faculty, practitioners, and students
- Foster excellence in teaching, research, and curriculum development for improving the education of human service delivery personnel
- Encourage, support, and assist the development of local, state, and national organizations for human service
- Sponsor forums through conferences, institutes, publications, and symposia that foster creative approaches to human service education and delivery

Services and Programs

- Community-support skill standards define the competencies used by direct-service workers in a wide variety of community settings, based on a nationally validated job analysis of a wide variety of human service workers, consumers, providers, and educators.
- Council for Standards in Human Service Education (CSHSE) published the *Ethical Standards of Human Service Professionals.*

Publications

Human Service Education: Annual journal.

Professional Credentialing

Accreditation for three levels of programs available through the Council for Standards in Human Service Education (see the section on Certifying and Accrediting Agencies and Academies, page 97).

▌ *Society for Nonprofit Organizations (SNPO)* ▐

Address

5820 Canton Center Rd., Ste. 165
Canton, MI 48187
phone: 734-451-3582
fax: 734-451-5935
e-mail: info@snpo.org
www.snpo.org

History

1983—Organization founded.

Mission and Goals

The mission of the SNPO is to promote the nonprofit sector through education, collaboration, and research in order to advance healthy and participatory communities.

Publications

Nonprofit World: Magazine published bimonthly.

Services and Programs

In 1996 the Learning Institute was established. Its educational programs are packaged into videotaped learning kits and include modules for individual and group presentation. The certificate series includes eight topics: board governance, marketing, mission-based management, resource development, social entrepreneurship, strategic alliances, strategic planning, and volunteer management. The enrichment series includes financial management, outcome measurement I and II, and planned giving.

NATURAL RESOURCES

This category has organizations with several different thrusts relating to natural resources and recreation. The first, American Zoo and Aquarium Association (AZA), is directed solely toward zoos and aquariums, while the next, National Society for Park Resources (NSPR), was established as a branch of National Recreation and Park Association (NRPA) principally for park professionals who work in municipal, county, regional, and state parks. The International Federation of Park and Recreation Administration (IFPRA) is an international organization for the same professionals. The resource planners organized under the National Association of Recreation Resource Planners (NARRP), while the park law enforcement professionals established the Park Law Enforcement Association (PLEA). You should be aware of two other professional organizations related to parks, National Association of State Park Directors (NASPD) and National Association of County Park and Recreation Officials (NACPRO), but because of their limited membership, they are not included in the descriptive detail of organizations. Then there is an active trade association related to campgrounds, the National Association of RV Parks and Campgrounds (ARVC). For interpretive services, see the section titled Outdoor Programming on page 69.

> AZA: American Zoo and Aquarium Association
> NSPR: National Society for Park Resources
> IFPRA: International Federation of Park and Recreation Administration
> NARRP: National Association of Recreation Resource Planners
> PLEA: Park Law Enforcement Association
> NASPD: National Association of State Park Directors, established 1962
> NACPRO: National Association of County Park and Recreation Officials
> ARVC: National Association of RV Parks and Campgrounds (www.arvc.org)

▌ *American Zoo and Aquarium Association (AZA)* ▌

Address

8403 Colesville Rd
Suite 710
Silver Springs, MD 20910-3314
phone: 301-562-0777
fax: 301-562-0888
e-mail: no general listing; see staff listing on Web site
www.aza.org

History

1924—founded as the American Association of Zoological Parks and Aquariums. (AAZPA was an affiliate of the American Institute of Park Executives, or AIPE.)

1966—AAZPA became a professional branch affiliate of the newly formed National Recreation and Park Association (NRPA) after 42 years of association with AIPE. AIPE was one of the merging organizations of the NRPA, and AAZPA went with it into the merger.

1971—AAZPA separated from NRPA and became an independent association.

1994—Changed acronym from AAZPA to AZA to enhance public visibility, but the actual name did not change.

Mission and Goals

AZA zoos and aquariums are places where people connect with animals. They are therefore dedicated to excellence in animal care and welfare, conservation, education, and research that constructively inspire respect for animals and nature. The mission of the professional association is to provide its members and their visitors with the best possible services through the following:

- Establishing and maintaining excellent professional standards in all AZA institutions through its accreditation program
- Establishing and promoting high standards of animal care and welfare
- Promoting and facilitating collaborative conservation and research programs
- Advocating effective governmental policies for members
- Strengthening and promoting conservation education programs for public and professional development for members
- Raising awareness of the collective impact of its members and their programs

Structural Organization

AZA has eight departments:
Conservation Education
Development and Marketing
Finance and Administration
Government Affairs
Conservation and Science
Membership Services
Public Affairs
Accreditation and Certification

Professional Credentialing

Accreditation of zoos is implemented by the AZA Accreditation Commission to ensure that institutions are providing their captive collections with appropriate levels of care, record keeping, veterinary care programs, education and conservation programs, security, and the aesthetic value of the facility. A zoo must be accredited to be a member of the AZA; accreditation is good for five years. International institutions may become accredited and members of AZA. AZA also has an extensive code of professional ethics, adopted in 1976, and an ethics board that handles complaints.

▌ *National Society for Park Resources (NSPR) (A branch of NRPA)* ▌

Address

National Society for Park Resources
c/o National Recreation and Park Association
22377 Belmont Ridge Rd.
Ashburn, VA 20148
phone: 703-858-0784
fax: 703-858-0794
e-mail: rdolesh@nrpa.org
www.nrpa.org/branches/nspr

History

1921—National Conference on State Parks (NCSP) was formed.

1956—NCSP joined with the National Park Service (NPS) to implement an innovative publication titled *Park Practice*.

1966—NCSP merged with the NRPA and became a branch.

1975—NCSP changed its name to the National Society for Park Resources (NSPR) and broadened its membership beyond state parks to include local parks as well as resource-oriented federal agencies.

1991—Adopted an environmental ethic statement of the Natural Resources Management Training Coalition (NRMTC) primary outreach and educational tool; members of coalition include NSPR, Armed Forces Recreation Society (AFRS), National Association of Recreation Resources Planners (NARRP), and National Association of State Park Directors (NASPD).

Mission and Goals

NPRS includes park, forest, and natural resource professionals who advance the art of planning, maintaining, interpreting, and administering resources of national, historic, and cultural value at all levels of government. The following is their professional creed:

- Dedication to resource protection through the use and improvement of accepted principles and practices of high-quality maintenance, resource reinvestment, and public information and education
- Accountability for the conservation of all resources, maintenance of all facilities, and excellence in public service programs

- Cooperation with other professionals and concerned citizens through positive sharing, persistence in outdoor conflict resolution, respect for all legitimate uses of the outdoors, and advocacy of outdoor values
- Responsibility for providing citizens with experiences designed to increase public awareness, understanding, and appreciation of our natural and cultural resources while also taking a lead role in advocating ecological and environmental concerns
- Competency in recreation resource stewardship reflected by continuing personal investment in professional growth through formal training and other educational opportunities

Publications

Park Practice, which includes four separate components (publications): *Trends, Design, Grist,* and *Guidelines* (in conjunction with National Park Service).

▍ *International Federation of Park and Recreation Administration (IFPRA)* ▍

Address

General Secretary of IFPRA
Globe House, Crispin Close
Caversham, Reading
England RG4 7JS
phone/fax: +44 (0) 118 946 1680
e-mail: ipraworld@aol.com
www.ifpra.org

History

1957—IFPRA established in London at time of first International Congress in Parks and Recreation.

Mission and Goals

Contacts throughout the world with national professional bodies and individuals representing parks, recreation, amenity, cultural, leisure, and related services.

Aims and objectives include the following:

- The advancement of parks, recreation, amenity, cultural, and leisure services through representation and dissemination of information
- The adoption of internationally acceptable training and qualification standards
- The promotion of relevant research
- The establishment of national recreation and park associations
- The promotion of the conservation ethic and the reduction of pollution
- The encouragement of efficient use of resources
- The organization of international congresses and meetings
- The publication of a bulletin
- The international exchange of students and professionals

Structural Organization

There are two regional sectors: Europe and Asia/Pacific.

| *National Association of Recreation Resource Planners (NARRP)* |

Address

NARRP
MSC-1777
P.O. Box 2430
Pensacola, FL 32513
e-mail: info@narrp.org
www.narrp.org

History

1981—The need for an organization was established at first nationwide conference of State Comprehensive Outdoor Recreation Plan (SCORP) planners.

1983—Organization formed as the National Association of State Recreation Planners (NASRP).

1994—Role of organization was expanded to cover broad range of outdoor recreation planning activities in both the public and private sectors; name changed to National Association of Recreation Resource Planners (NARRP).

Mission and Goals

To advance the art, the science, and the profession of outdoor recreation planning to enhance outdoor recreation opportunities for all Americans. To provide professional development, NARRP participates in the National Resources Management Training Coalition with National Association of State Park Directors, National Society of Park Resources, and Armed Forces Recreation Society.

Objectives include the following:

• To exchange recreation planning and related information
• To promote the professional growth of individuals involved in recreation planning
• To develop and voice unified positions on recreation planning concerns
• To promote member services in the areas of education, research, public relations, and public and private practice

| *Park Law Enforcement Association (PLEA) (An affiliate of the NRPA)* |

Address

Park Law Enforcement Association
c/o National Recreation and Park Association
22377 Belmont Ridge Road
Ashburn, VA 20148
phone: 877-PARKLAW; 703-858-0784
fax: 703-858-0794
e-mail: info@nrpa.org
www.parkranger.com

History

1984—founded.

Mission and Goals

PLEA members include park rangers, forest rangers, park patrols, park police, park security, game wardens, conservation officers, park or recreation board members, administrators, educators, and other interested park and recreation professionals.

PLEA's mission is to improve law enforcement development, thus better assuring quality of life at leisure opportunities in local, state, and national park and recreation areas. The organization's goal is to provide public visibility, continuing education and training, technical assistance, research, accreditation, and programming and marketing ideas to members of the park and recreation profession.

Professional Credentialing

No credentialing services. However, law enforcement agencies may be accredited by the Commission on Accreditation for Law Enforcement.

OUTDOOR PROGRAMMING

The organizations in this category focus on programming using the natural environment in organized camping, adventure and challenge, environmental education, and interpretive services.

Three primary organizations are related to organized camping.

ACA: American Camping Association

CCCA: Christian Camp and Conference Association

CCA: Canadian Camping Association

The International Camping Fellowship (ICF) has the primary purpose of holding an international congress every three to four years. The second congress was held in 1987 in Washington, DC. More than 1,800 people attended from 15 different countries. Its address is ICF, R.R. 1, Huntsville, ON, Canada, P1H 2J2; phone: 705-789-5612, e-mail: icf@campingfellowship.org.

In addition, some associations focus on camping for selected populations, such as people with disabilities or specific illnesses (e.g., diabetes), members of religious organizations (e.g., Catholics), or members of particular professions (e.g., Association for Camp Nurses, Christian Camping Horsemanship International). For information on RV and campground camping, see www.arvc.org.

Outdoor adventure and challenge programs are the focus of five organizations; however two, Association of Outdoor Recreation and Education (AORE) and Council for Adventure and Outdoor Education/Recreation (CAOER), include both adventure and challenge programs and environmental education:

AEE: Association for Experiential Education

WEA: Wilderness Education Association

ACCT: Association for Challenge Course Technology (a trade association, but membership open to individuals)

AORE: Association of Outdoor Recreation and Education

CAOER: Council for Adventure and Outdoor Education/Recreation

Environmental education is the primary focus of three organizations.

ANSS: American Nature Study Society

CEO: Coalition for Education in the Outdoors

NAAEE: North American Association for Environmental Education

Detailed information for the National Marine Educators Association (NMEA) has not been included here, because it has a particular focus; however, with the importance of water and wetlands, it should be considered an environmental education resource. For more information, see its Web site: www.marine-ed.org.

Four organizations focus on interpretive services.

NAI: National Association for Interpretation

Interpretation Canada

VSA: Visitor Studies Association

ANCA: Association of Nature Center Administrators

Historical and cultural programs and services have become an important aspect of the interpretive services field, and NAI, VSA, and Interpretation Canada offer opportunities related to these aspects. American Association of State and Local History (AASLH) is an organization primarily for historians, but offers an excellent opportunity to the recreation and parks professional interested in community cultural history and the development of community museums. Two other organizations, Association for Heritage Interpretation (AHI) and Association for Living History, Farms and Agricultural Museums (ALHFAM) may also be useful to the recreation and parks professional interested in this area.

AASLH: American Association of State and Local History (www.aaslh.org)

AHI: Association for Heritage Interpretation (www.heritageinterpretation.org. uk)

ALHFAM: Association for Living History, Farms and Agricultural Museums (www.alhfam.org)

Finally, a number of organizations have a special focus. These are the International Consortium for Experiential Learning (ICEL) (www.el.uct.ac.za/icel/), National Association of Therapeutic Wilderness Camps (NATWC) (www.natwc.org), and a trade association, Professional Paddlesports Association (PPA) (www.propaddle.com).

▌ *American Camping Association (ACA)* ▌

Address

5000 State Rd. 67 N
Martinsville, IN 46151-7902
phone: 765-342-8456
fax: 765-342-2065
e-mail: membership@ACAcamps.org (see Web site for addresses for specific services)
www.acacamps.org

History

1910—Founded as the Camp Directors' Association of America.

1935—The name changed to the American Camping Association.

1948—Camp standards were officially adopted.

1957—Campcraft certification program established; now Outdoor Living Skills (OLS).

1996—The private independent camp, kindred group, was separately incorporated as a trade association and became an ACA-affiliated organization

Mission and Goals

The mission of the American Camping Association is to form a community of camp professionals dedicated to enriching the lives of children and adults through the camp experience.

The organization's purpose is as follows:

- Serve as a knowledge center
- Educate camp owners and directors in the administration of camp operations, particularly program quality, health, and safety
- Assist the public in selecting camps that meet industry-accepted and goverment-recognized standards

Structural Organization

For many years ACA served organizations and settings by providing organized camping through kindred groups. In an extensive bylaws revision, the structural organization was changed to provide for three ACA-affiliated organizations:

- AIC: Association of Independent Camps (separately incorporated in 1996 as a trade association; see www.independentcamps.com)
- Not-for-Profit Council and Not-for-Profit Forum (open to any ACA member with not-for-profit organization affiliation; the council is the facilitating body and is composed of one representative from each section of the ACA, three elected officers, and three members at large; see www.acacamps.org/nfpc)
- RAC: Religiously Affiliated Camp Council (open to any ACA member interested in interfaith networking; see www.acacamps.org/rac)

Several kindred groups, such as the Association of Camp Nurses and the Salvation Army, still exist. They meet at the time of national ACA convention, as do the three affiliated organizations. Members of the kindred groups and the affiliated organizations participate actively in ACA convention sessions and activities.

Services and Programs

See the organization's Web site for an extensive list of services. The following are a few examples:

- Professional development courses
- Information about legislative issues and public policy regarding child safety and protection
- Camp management center referral and consultation
- Industry public awareness program

Publications

Camping Magazine: Published six times a year.

Professional Credentialing

ACA has an extensive accreditation program, which is implemented through a National Standards Commission (see the section on Certifying and Accrediting Agencies and Academies, page 97). This includes the accreditation of camp programs and services (organized day and resident camps and sites) and accreditation of conference and retreat centers. ACA also has developed a code of ethics.

| *Christian Camp and Conference Association (CCCA)* |

Address

CCCA
P.O. Box 62189
Colorado Springs, CO 80962-2189
phone: 719-260-9400
fax: 719-260-6398
e-mail: info@ccca-us.org
www.gospelcom.net/cci

History

1940s and 50s—Several regional groups of Christian camp and Bible conference leaders in the United States and Canada began to meet informally. These coalitions later combined their efforts under the name Christian Camp and Conference Association International (CCCAI).

1963—CCCAI incorporated and changed its name to Christian Camping International (CCI).

2005—Changed name to Christian Camp and Conference Association (CCCA).

Mission and Goals

Christian Camp and Conference Association aims to protect ministry vision. Because a host of outside pressures can divert attention from goals and objectives, CCCA is committed to keeping its members focused on the primary mission of shaping lives. An alliance of 14 Christian camping associations help one another develop effective Christ-centered camps, conference, and retreat ministries. Each association has its own programs to accomplish the mission objectives and to accomplish its own national and regional objectives.

CCCA goals include the following:

- Increase public awareness. By maintaining a presence in the Christian community and by representing its membership to the public, CCCA uniquely speaks for the entire movement and continually affirms the viability of Christian camps and conferences.

- Promote industry excellence. CCCA is committed to helping its members, individually and collectively, to meet and exceed marketplace standards, and to attain excellence in programming, facility management, staffing, and operations.

- Provide networking opportunities. CCCA helps members grow personally and professionally, and thus encourages and expedites various types of interaction in order to maintain a vast program of mutual support.

- Expand ministry horizons. Possibilities abound outside the gates of every camp and conference. CCCA is compelled to introduce members to creative methods and special populations—at home and abroad—who will benefit from an outdoor ministry experience or from being in a Christian hospitality setting.

Structural Organization

CCCA is an association composed of 18 autonomous associations on six continents. CCCA is the largest association. See also Christian Camping Horsemanship International (CCHI) www.instructors4christ.org.

Publications

Christian Camp & Conference Journal.

| *Canadian Camping Association (CCA)* |

Address

Box 74030
Edmonton, AB, Canada T5K 2S7
phone: (toll free) 877-427-6958 or 780-427-6605
fax: 780-427-6695
e-mail: info@ccamping.org
www.ccamping.org

History

1950—Representatives of Provincial Camping Associations (PCAs) met to form the CCA.

Mission and Goals

CCA's mission is to be a national federation dedicated to the growth, development, and promotion of organized camping for all populations in Canada.

Structural Organization

CCA is a federation of eight provincial camping associations. Individuals should take membership in the appropriate provincial association. See the CCA Web site for provincial contacts.

Services and Programs

See the organization's Web site for an extensive list of special services. Here are a few examples:

- National statistics and market research
- Media package and public awareness
- National insurance program

Professional Credentialing

Each provincial association has developed standards. In 2001 CCA convened a national workshop to share the differences and similarities.

❙ *Association for Experiential Education (AEE)* ❙

Address

3775 Iris, Ste.4
Boulder, CO 80301-2043
phone: 303-440-8844
866-522-8337
fax: 303-440-9581
e-mail: executive@aee.org (see Web site for e-mail of specific services)
www.aee.org

History

1973—First Conference on Outdoor Pursuits in Higher Education was held.

1977—AEE was incorporated.

1996—Council on Accreditation of Adventure Programs established.

Mission and Goals

AEE's vision is to contribute to making a more just and compassionate world by transforming education.

AEE's mission is to develop and promote experiential education. The association is committed to support professional development, theoretical advancement, and evaluation of experiential education worldwide.

Structural Organization

The association is organized into six professional groups (PGs). This provides opportunity for members to affiliate with others who share similar professional interests and endeavors within experiential education. The groups are as follows:

- Experience-based training and development (EBTD)
- Gays, lesbians, bisexuals, and allies (LGBA)
- Natives, Africans, Asians, Latino(a)s, and allies (NAALA)
- Schools and colleges (S&C)
- Therapeutic adventure (TAPG)
- Women in experiential education (WPG)

Services and Programs

The association conducted an Outcome Measurement Survey in 2002. Results and assessment instruments are available.

Publications

Journal of Experiential Education: Published three times a year.

Professional Credentialing

The Council on Accreditation of Adventure Programs was established in 1996 (see the section on Certifying and Accrediting Agencies and Academies, page 97).

Wilderness Education Association (WEA)

Address

Indiana University
900 E. 7th St.
Bloomington, IN 47405
phone: 812-855-4095
fax: 812-855-8697
e-mail: info@weainfo.org
www.weainfo.org

History

1977—WEA founded to train outdoor leaders through a decentralized approach via the academic community.

Mission and Goals

WEA's mission is to promote the professionalism of outdoor leadership to thereby improve the safety of outdoor trips and to enhance the conservation of the wild outdoors.

Structural Organization

Thirty college, camp, and agency affiliates conduct educational courses.

Services and Programs

The wilderness steward program is an 18-point curriculum taught through a network of accredited colleges and affiliated outdoor organizations.

Publications

WEA Legend: Published quarterly.

Professional Credentialing

WEA administers the Certified Wilderness Instructor program.

Association for Challenge Course Technology (ACCT)

Address

P.O. Box 255
Martin, MI 49070-0255
phone: 269-685-0670
fax: 269-685-6350
e-mail: acct@net-link.net (see Web site for e-mail addresses for various services)
www.acctinfo.org

History

1988—Concept began with a series of ropes course builder symposia.

1993—Organization formally organized.

Mission and Goals

ACCT is a trade association open to individual members. The organization's purpose is to promote the use of challenge courses and to set minimum standards for challenge-course installation, operation, and safety inspections.

The organization's mission is to establish and guide the implementation and compliance of standards. These standards promote quality and safety for the installation, inspection, and operation of and promote ethical practices by vendors and institutional and individual member program providers. The organization is committed to developing and advancing challenge-course technology through the research of industry and member resources.

Services and Programs

The organization has established standards that detail common and recommended practices in challenge-course construction, inspection, and operation.

Publications

Parallel Lines: Published three times a year.

Professional Credentialing

The organization has developed ACCT challenge-course standards; however, this is not an accreditation program.

Association of Outdoor Recreation and Education (AORE)

Address

2705 Robin St.
Bloomington, IL 61704
phone and fax: 309-829-9189
e-mail: nationaloffice@aore.org
www.aore.org

History

1993—Organization established.

Mission and Goals

AORE's mission is to provide opportunities for professionals and students in the field of outdoor recreation and education to exchange information, promote the preservation and conservation of the natural environment, and address issues common to college, university, community, military, and other not-for-profit outdoor recreation and education programs.

The following are AORE's goals:

- Serve the needs of the association membership and constituency
- Encourage and facilitate the exchange of ideas and information in the profession
- Support ecologically sound stewardship of the outdoor environment
- Serve as the collective voice for association membership on topics of local, regional, national, and international concern

See AORE's Web site for objectives for each goal.

Structural Organization

AORE's annual conference is the International Conference on Outdoor Recreation and Education (ICORE).

Services and Programs

AORE, in partnership with NIRSA, promotes opportunities in outdoor recreation and education.

Council for Adventure and Outdoor Education/Recreation (CAOER)

A unit of AAHPERD

Address

CAOER
1900 Association Dr.
Reston, VA 20191
phone: 800-213-7193
fax: 703-476-9527
e-mail: See Web site for most up-to-date contact
www.aahperd.org (search for CAOER)

History

1940—Outdoor Education Association (OEA) founded.

1955—An extensive outdoor education project was initiated under AAHPERD.

1965—Council on Outdoor Education was established (under Recreation Division of AAHPERD).

1985—NASPE approved adventure and challenge activities as an acceptable part of physical education under its standards.

2003—CAOER established as AALR interest area.

2005—CAOER became a council under AAPAR merging AAALF's Council on Outdoor Education and AALR's interest group.

Mission and Goals

The Council on Outdoor Education's mission is to support professionals who work in higher education, elementary schools, secondary schools, recreation and park programs, and clinical settings who provide programs in, for, and about the out-of-doors. Particular emphasis is placed on team building through the use of ropes and adventure courses.

Structural Organization

Council under AAPAR, an association of AAHPERD.

Services and Programs

- A partnership between AAPAR (formerly AALR) and WEA offers wilderness leadership training for educator workshops.
- Through a major grant in 2003 from the Recreational Boating and Fishing Foundation and Future Fisherman Foundation, AAPAR (formerly AALR) and NASPE provide fishing and boating education.

| *American Nature Study Society (ANSS)* |

Address

c/o Pocono Environmental Education Center (PEEC)
RR 2, Box 1010
Dinghams Ferry, PA 18328
phone: 570-828-2319
fax: 570-828-9695
e-mail: anssonline@aol.com
www.hometown.aol.com/anssonline

History

1908—Organization founded. It is the oldest environmental education organization in the United States.

Mission and Goals

The American Nature Study Society's mission is to promote effective education and environmental literacy.

Publications

Nature Study.

| *Coalition for Education in the Outdoors (CEO)* |

Address

State University of New York at Cortland
P.O. Box 2000, Park Center
Cortland, NY 13045
phone: 607-753-4971
fax: 607-753-5982
e-mail: info@outdooredcoalition.org
www.outdooredcoalition.org

History

1987—Organization founded.
1992—First CEO research symposium held.

Mission and Goals

CEO's mission is to support and further outdoor education and its goals. Goals include personal growth and moral development, team building and cooperation, outdoor knowledge and skill development, and environmental awareness, education, and enrichment.

Structural Organization

The organization is a network of outdoor and environmental education centers, nature centers, conservation and recreation organizations, outdoor education and experiential education associations, institutions of higher learning, public and private schools, fish and wildlife agencies, and businesses. Individuals also may join.

Services and Programs

The organization conducts a biennial research symposium.

Publications

Research Symposia Proceedings: Published biennially.

Taproot: Journal published quarterly.

| *North American Association for Environmental Education (NAAEE)* |

Address

2000 P Street NW, Ste. 540
Washington, DC 20036
phone: 202-419-0412
fax: 202-419-0415
e-mail: email@naaee.org
www.naaee.org

History

1947—The Conservation Education Association (CEA) was founded.

1971—Organization founded as National Association for Environmental Education (NAEE).

1983—Changed name to North American Association for Environmental Education (NAAEE).

1990—CEA merged into NAAEE, but retained identity as a section (now a commission).

Mission and Goals

Since 1971, the association has promoted environmental education and supported the work of environmental educators. Many organizations are dedicated to improving education; NAAEE uniquely combines and integrates both education and environmental concerns, and takes a cooperative, nonconfrontational, scientific-balanced approach to promoting education about environmental issues.

NAAEE is made up of people who have thought seriously about how people become literate in environmental issues. NAAEE members believe education must go beyond raising consciousness about these issues. It must prepare people to think together about the difficult decisions they have to make concerning environmental stewardship and to work together to improve and try to solve environmental problems.

NAAEE recognizes the need for a coherent body of information about environmental issues. Its members also recognize that information and analysis are only part of an effective education program. To be truly effective, the body of knowledge must be integrated into all aspects of the curriculum and into all types of educating institutions for the widest array of audiences.

Structural Organization

The association is organized into six commissions established for members with an interest in a particular professional area. Following are the areas:

- Conservation
- Elementary and Secondary Education
- Nonformal
- Higher Education
- Research
- International

Services and Programs

NAAEE's mission is to translate theory into practice and to provide support or environmental education and educators. The organization offers a variety of programs and activities.

- In 1995 NAAEE was named manager of the Environmental Education and Training Partnership (EETAP 1) funded by the Environmental Protection Agency (EPA). In 1999 it became a partner with University of Wisconsin–Stevens Point for EETAP 2 (see www.eetap.org).
- In 1996, with the National Project for Excellence in Environmental Education, began publishing a series of guideline documents, including guidelines for evaluating environmental education materials and guidelines that draw from standards in subject areas to define comprehensive kindergarten through 12th grade environmental education programs.

Publications

NAAEE Communicator.

Recent Graduate Works in Environmental Education and Communications: Since 1977 theses and doctoral dissertations published annually.

| *National Association for Interpretation (NAI)* |

Address

NAI National Office
528 S. Howes
Fort Collins, CO 80522
or
P.O. Box 2246
Fort Collins, CO 80521
phone: 888-900-8283 (toll free) or 970-484-8283
fax: 970-484-8179
e-mail: naiexec@aol.com
www.interpnet.com

History

1893—The American Society of Naturalists (ASN) was founded.

196l—ASN became the Association of Interpretive Naturalists (AIN).

1988—AIN and the Western Interpreters Association (WIA) merged to form the National Association for Interpretation.

Mission and Goals

The mission of NAI is to inspire leadership and excellence to advance natural and cultural interpretation as a profession.

Structural Organization

Eleven subject matter networks provide networking opportunities among members with similar interests:

- African-American experience
- College and university academics
- Council for the interpretation of native peoples
- Cultural interpretation and living history
- Environmental education
- Interpretive naturalist
- Interpretation and tourism
- Nature center directors and administrators
- Spanish
- Visual communications
- Zoos, wildlife parks, and aquaria

Publications

Legacy: Published six times a year.

Journal of Interpretation Research: Published annually.

Professional Credentialing

The NAI's professional certification program, initiated in 1997, consists of the following six categories:

- Certified heritage interpreter (CHI)
- Certified interpretive manager (CIM)
- Certified interpretive planner (CIP)
- Certified interpretive trainer (CIT)
- Certified interpretive guide (CIG) for volunteers, seasonal workers, and new hires who deliver programs or have public contact at interpretive sites but with no previous training in interpretation
- Certified interpretive host (CIH) also for volunteers, seasonal workers, and new hires, as well as maintenance workers, receptionists, and law enforcement employees who have public contact but do not deliver presentations

Certification is valid for four years; recertification requires 40 hours of additional training over the four years.

▎ *Interpretation Canada* ▎

Address

c/o Kerry Wood Nature Centre
6300 45th Ave.
Red Deer, AB, Canada T4N 3M4
No phone number available
fax: 604-648-8757
e-mail: membership@interpcan.ca
www.interpcan.ca

History

1973—First gathering to establish organization.

Publications

Interpscan: Published quarterly.

Visitor Studies Association (VSA)

Address

8175-A Sheridan Blvd., Ste. 362
Arvada, CO 80003-1928
phone: 303-467-2200
fax: 303-467-0064
e-mail: info@visitorstudies.org
www.visitorstudies.org

History

1992—Organization incorporated.

Mission and Goals

The Visitor Studies Association is an international network of professionals committed to understanding and enhancing visitor experiences in informal learning settings through research, valuation, and dialogue.

Structural Organization

The association is divided into the following five fields of interest:

- Visitor orientation
- Exhibit and program evaluation
- Development of methodology for visitor studies
- Visitor surveys and audience development
- Evaluation of visitor services

Publications

Visitor Studies Today!: Research-based publication, published three times a year.

Association of Nature Center Administrators (ANCA)

Address

Aullwood Audubon Center and Farm
1000 Aullwood Rd.
Dayton, OH 45414
phone: 800-490-2622
fax: 937-890-2382
e-mail: lbrown@audubon.org
www.natctr.org

History

1987—Founded and operated as an affiliate of the National Institute for Urban Wildlife.

1993—Incorporated as independent membership organization.

Mission and Goals

ANCA's mission is to promote and support leadership and management practices for the nature and environmental learning center profession.

The following are the association's goals:

- Establish a national network for nature center administrators
- Promote the identity and professional stature of nature center educational facilities
- Provide nature center administrators with products and services that will improve their performance on the job

Publications

The Director's Guide to Best Practices.

COMMERCIAL RECREATION AND TOURISM

This category is composed of three major types of organizations: (a) organizations that serve employees of a given business, (b) organizations whose focus is travel and tourism, and (c) organizations that serve the resort and commercial recreation field, including selected trade associations that serve specific aspects of the commercial recreation field. The field of travel and tourism, as an emphasis in the recreation and park academic curriculum, is relatively new, with impetus in the 1990s. The organizations described in this category are those that educators in the field associate with and that students look to for jobs. Many other organizations are related to travel and tourism and to the resort and commercial recreation field. If you are a student, your professors may provide more information about these organizations. Most of the organizations Web sites have links to other organizations.

Employee recreation has been around for many years, but it became become more important at the beginning of the 21st century with the focus on employee health and health care costs. The principal employee organization is ESM Association.

ESM Association: Employee Services Management Association

There is no general membership organization focus in travel and tourism. The closest is the Travel and Tourism Research Association (TTRA) or the educator association, International Society of Travel and Tourism Educators (ISTTE). There are, however, several special focus organizations and several councils: IACVB, MPI, IFEA, IAAM, and IAAPA. There are also several councils, such as WTTC, WTO, and the Canadian Tourism Commission. Hotel and restaurant associations, although part of the travel and tourism hospitality industry, are not included; see the *Directory of Trade and Professional Organizations* for listings.

TTRA: Travel and Tourism Research Association

ISTTE: International Society of Travel and Tourism Educators

IACVB: International Association of Convention and Visitor Bureaus

MPI: Meeting Professionals International

IFEA: International Festivals & Events Association

IAAM: International Association of Assembly Managers

IAAPA: International Association of Amusement Parks and Attractions

WTTC: World Travel and Tourism Council (www.wttc.org)

WTO: World Tourism Organization (www.world-tourism.org)

CTC: Canadian Tourism Commission (www.canadatourism.com)

Resort and Commercial Recreation Association (RCRA) and Commercial Recreation and Tourism Section (CRTS) are two general commercial recreation organizations. However, some trade organizations have a special focus, such as IHRSA, PPA, and ARVC. Most offer individual memberships and welcome students to their conferences. North American Society for Sport Management (NASSM) is concerned with managing sport in both commercial and noncommercial settings. Refer to the *Directory of Trade and Professional Organizations* for others with a specific area of focus.

RCRA: Resort and Commercial Recreation Association

CRTS: Commercial Recreation and Tourism Section (a section of NRPA)

IHRSA: International Health, Racquet, and Sportsclub Association (see page 96)

PPA: Professional Paddlers Association (www.propaddle.com)

ARVC: National Association of RV Parks and Campgrounds (see section on Natural Resources, page 64)

NASSM: North American Society for Sport Management (see section on Recreation, page 46)

Employee Services Management Association (ESM Association)

Address

2211 York Rd., Ste. 207
Oak Brook, IL 60523-2371
phone: 630-368-1280
fax: 630-368-1286
e-mail: esmahq@esmassn.org
www.esmassn.org

History

1941—Founded as the National Industrial Recreation Association (NIRA).

1951—The American Recreation Society (ARS) Industrial Recreation Section was founded.

1966—The ARS, but not NIRA, merged into the NRPA, and the new NRPA did not provide a branch for industrial recreation (employee recreation).

1982—NIRA changed its name to the National Employee Services and Recreation Association (NESRA).

2000—NESRA changed its name to Employee Services Management Association (ESMA).

Structural Organization

ESM Association Education and Research Foundation was created to collect funds that support research.

Publications

ESM Magazine: Published monthly.

Professional Credentialing

Certified Employee Services Manager (CESM)

Travel and Tourism Research Association (TTRA)

Address

P.O. Box 2133
Boise, ID 83701
phone: 208-429-9511
fax: 208-429-9512
e-mail: info@ttra.com
www.ttra.com

History

1970—Association founded.

Mission and Goals

TTRA's mission is to serve as a primary resource to the travel and tourism industry, advocate standards, and promote the application of quality travel and tourism research.

Publications

Journal of Travel Research: Published quarterly.

Professional Credentialing

TTRA supports the Principles of Marketing Research certificate program.

International Society of Travel and Tourism Educators (ISTTE)

Address

23220 Edgewater
St. Clair Shores, MI 48082
phone and fax: 586-294-0208
e-mail: istte@aol.com
www.istte.org

History

1971—Society founded.

Mission and Goals

ISTTE's mission is to represent teachers and administrators in high schools, proprietary schools, community colleges, four-year colleges, and graduate programs. It focuses on providing training for the men and women who will enter some part of the travel and tourism industry.

Publications

Journal of Teaching in Travel & Tourism.

▌ *International Association of Convention & Visitor Bureaus (IACVB)* ▌

Address

2025 M Street NW, Ste. 500
Washington, DC 20036
phone: 202-296-7888
fax: 202-296-7889
e-mail: info@iacvb.org
www.iacvb.org

History

1914—Association founded.

Mission and Goals

IACVB's mission is to enhance the professionalism, effectiveness, and image of destination management organizations worldwide.

Services and Programs

Performance Measurement Initiative

▌ *Meeting Professionals International (MPI)* ▌

Address

International Headquarters
4455 LBJ Freeway, Ste. 1700
Dallas, TX 75234-2759
phone: 972-702-3000
fax: 972-702-3070
e-mail: ms@mpiweb.org (see Web site for e-mail addresses for various services)
www.mpiweb.org

Canadian Office
6519-B Mississauga Rd.
Mississauga, ON, Canada L5N 1A6
phone: 905-286-4807
fax: 905-567-7191
e-mail: mpicanada@mpiweb.org
www.mpiweb.org

History

1972—Organization established.

Mission and Goals

MPI will be recognized as the leading global membership community committed to shaping and defining the meeting and event industry.

Structural Organization

The MPI Foundation was founded in 1984 to collect funds for conducting research and developing projects to improve the meeting planning process, function, and management.

Publications

The Meeting Professional.

Professional Credentialing

MPI offers three certifications:

- Certified Meeting Professional (CMP)
- Certification in Meeting Management (CMM)
- Meeting Professionals International's Principles of Professionalism

International Festivals & Events Association (IFEA)

Address

2601 Eastover Terrace
Boise, ID 83706
phone: 208-433-0950
fax: 208-433-9812
e-mail: nia@iefa.com (see Web site for e-mail addresses for various services)
www.ifea.com

History

1956—Founded as International Festivals Association.

1997—Name changed to International Festivals & Events Association.

Mission and Goals

IFEA members include individuals employed by the administrations of community and civic festivals.

Services and Programs

The IFEA has developed an economic impact study (EIS) model that provides economic impact and demographic information.

Publications

IE: The Business of International Events: Published quarterly.

Professional Credentialing

IFEA administers the Certified Festival & Event Executive (CFEE) program. The association has developed a code of professional conduct and ethics and a code of professional responsibility.

❙ *International Association of Assembly Managers (IAAM)* ❙

Address

635 Fritz Dr., Ste. 100
Coppell, TX 75019
phone: 972-906-7441
fax: 972-906-7418
e-mail: iaamwhq@iaam.org
(for membership; also see Web site for e-mail addresses for various services)
www.iaam.org

History

1924—Founded as Auditorium Managers' Association (AMA).

Mission and Goals

IAAM's mission is to provide leadership, to educate, to inform, and to cultivate friendships among individuals involved in the management, operation, and support of public assembly facilities. The association's overall goal is to contribute to the professional and personal development of public assembly facility manager members through promotion and development of quality programs and services.

The following are the association's objectives:

- Promote and develop professional management of public assembly facilities
- Foster use of these facilities for the benefit, recreation, and entertainment of the public
- Cultivate acquaintance and communication among facility managers
- Circulate information of value to the members and the public in order to develop more frequent and efficient facility use
- Standardize practices and ethics of management and relationships with the public
- Develop and maintain liaison with national and international organizations in allied fields
- Advance the association

Structural Organization

The IAAM Foundation was established in 1982, as a 501c(3) nonprofit organization, to fund educational programs, professional development, and research.

Publications

Facility Manager: Bimonthly magazine.

Professional Credentialing

Certified Facilities Executive (CFE)

▮ *International Association of Amusement Parks and Attractions (IAAPA)* ▮

Address

1448 Duke St.
Alexandria, VA 22314
phone: 703-836-4800
fax: 703-836-9678
e-mail: membership@iaapa.org (see Web site for e-mail addresses for specific service or staff)
www.iaapa.org

History

1918—Association founded.

Mission and Goals

IAAPA exists to foster the highest degree of professionalism within the amusement industry, to promote the market for its goods and services, to gather and disseminate information about the industry, and to represent the interests of the industry before government—all to the end that our member companies grow and profit.

Publications

Funworld: Published monthly.

Professional Credentialing

The association has developed a code of ethics.

▮ *Resort and Commercial Recreation Association (RCRA)* ▮

Address

P.O. Box 4327
Sunriver, OR 97707
phone: 541-593-3711
fax: 541-593-7833
e-mail: info@r-c-r-a.org
www.r-c-r-a.org

History

1981—Founded by a group to create a network for sharing ideas in an emerging field.

Mission and Goals

RCRA's purpose as a nonprofit organization is to further the resort and commercial recreation industries through appropriate services to professionals, educators, and students and to increase the profitability of commercial enterprises with a recreation focus.

The association's goals include the following:

- Establish an effective and functional national vehicle to communicate, educate, disseminate, and promote professionalism within the industry

- Involve all facets of the industry
- Provide opportunity for continuing education related to the industry

Structural Organization

RCRA membership represents the following key commercial recreation interests: theme parks, hotel and convention centers, concessionaires, travel and tourism, resorts, private industries, campgrounds, vendors, health clubs, and universities.

Publications

Resort + Recreation Magazine.

Professional Credentialing

The Professional Certification Council administers the Certified Commercial Recreation Professional (CCRP) program.

Commercial Recreation and Tourism Section (CRTS)

A section of NRPA

Address

c/o NRPA
22377 Belmont Ridge Rd.
Ashburn, VA 20148-4150
phone: 703-858-0784
fax: 703-858-0794
e-mail: dvaira@nrpa.org
www.nrpa.org (select About NRPA, then Branches and Sections)

Mission and Goals

CRTS's goals include the following:

- Become the national professional organization for individuals concerned with the advancement and growth of the commercial recreation and tourism industry
- Involve all people associated with commercial recreation and tourism
- Provide an opportunity for continued education related to commercial recreation and tourism
- Work with the structure of NRPA and in cooperation with all of its sections and branches
- Encourage universities, colleges, and other institutions to promulgate and disseminate knowledge about commercial recreation and tourism

THERAPEUTIC RECREATION, DISABILITIES, AND FITNESS

This category includes organizations that serve three related professional fields: (a) use of recreation for therapeutic purposes in clinical and community settings,

(b) engagement of people with various disabilities (previously referred to as special populations) in activity, and (c) fitness programs.

Three principal professional organizations serve therapeutic recreation. Because of its focus on activity professionals in geriatric settings, a fourth organization, National Association of Activity Professionals (NAAP), has been included.

NTRS: National Therapeutic Recreation Society

ATRA: American Therapeutic Recreation Association

CTRA: Canadian Therapeutic Recreation Association

NAAP: National Association of Activity Professionals

Adapted physical activity, especially sport, has long been a part of adapted physical education (see part II). However, because adapted physical education is usually a part of the school physical education program, specific physical education professional organizations are not described here (see the listing for AAHPERD, page 47).

Sport is an integral part of activity for people with disabilities, and more through adapted physical education than recreation. However, with the implementation of the Americans with Disabilities Act, recreation professionals have had to be more involved with physical activity and sport for people with disabilities in their regular program offerings.

Many organizations have been established to focus on sport for people with specific disabilities. More than 85 of these organizations in the United States and Canada are listed in *Disability and Sport,* Second Edition (2005). These generally are not considered professional organizations, but broad-based organizations with which recreation professionals work. Therefore, they are not individually included and described here. One general organization for adapted physical activity is detailed here:

IFAPA: International Federation of Adapted Physical Activity.

Organizations also exist for activities other than sport, such as the National Association of Therapeutic Wilderness Camps (NATWC, www.natwc.org) and North American Riding for the Handicapped Association (NARHA, www.narha.org). Both are considered professional organizations, and recreation professionals working with these activities should belong.

The third aspect, fitness, also has historically been the domain of health and physical education, including athletic training. Fitness staff usually have academic backgrounds in health and physical education. However, beginning in the mid-90s, when recreation curricula emphasized management, and health and fitness clubs were popular, universities offered courses in health club management, but the curricula did not include the substantive element of health and fitness.

Two organizations are detailed: American College of Sport Medicine (ACSM), which focuses primarily on the substantive aspects of fitness, and International Health, Racquet, and Sportsclubs Association (IHRSA), which focuses principally on club management. IHRSA is a trade association with membership for clubs, not individuals.

ACSM: American College of Sports Medicine

IHRSA: International Health, Racquet & Sportsclubs Association

Many organizations, particularly for instructors, focus on a specific aspect of fitness, such as aerobics and weight training (see the *Directory of Trade and Professional Organizations*).

| *National Therapeutic Recreation Society (NTRS)* |

A branch of NRPA

Address

c/o NRPA
22377 Belmont Ridge Rd.
Ashburn, VA 20148-4150
phone: 703-858-0784
fax: 703-858-0794
e-mail: ntrsnrpa@nrpa.com
www.nrpa.org (select About NRPA, then Branches and Sections)

History

1954—Council for Advancement of Hospital Recreation (CAHR) formed.

1966—Four organizations merged to form NTRS as a branch of NRPA:

Hospital Recreation Section of American Recreation Society (ARS): founded 1948

Recreation Therapist Section of AAHPERD: founded 1952

National Association of Recreation Therapists (NART): founded 1953

NRA Recreation Services for the Handicapped: established 1953

1978—NTRS registration program recognized for therapeutic recreation personnel.

1979—Guidelines for Community-Based Recreation Programs for Special Populations, Standards of Practice for Therapeutic Recreation Services, and Guidelines for Administration of Therapeutic Recreation Service in Clinical and Residential Facilities were developed.

1996—A joint task force on credentialing was formed between NTRS and ATRS.

Mission and Goals

NTRS provides members the opportunity to enhance their competence and their commitment. Members create and personalize a network of support, information, and action designed to articulate the practice and benefits of the therapeutic recreation profession. Members energetically and creatively provide and receive inspiration, friendship, and mentoring opportunities for professional growth and an open forum for the exchange of ideas in an atmosphere of mutual respect.

Publications

Therapeutic Recreation Journal: Published quarterly.

Standards of Practice: Approved by NTRS Board in 2000.

Professional Credentialing

Members participate in National Council for Therapeutic Recreation Certification (NCTRC) certificate program (see the section on Certifying and Accrediting Agencies and Academies, page 97).

▍ *American Therapeutic Recreation Association (ATRA)* ▍

Address

1414 Prince St., Ste. 204
Alexandra, VA 22314
phone: 703-683-9420
fax: 703-683-9431
e-mail: atra@arta-tr.org
www.atra-tr.org

History

1984—Founded as a nonprofit organization designed to advance the needs of therapeutic recreation professionals in health care and human service settings.

1996—A joint task force on credentialing formed between NTRS and ATRS.

Mission and Goals

The purpose of the association is to further the objectives set forth in the articles of incorporation by serving as an advocate for therapeutic recreation in order to promote the health and well-being of the public through service, education, research, and the development and enforcement of standards.

Publications

ATRA Annual in Therapeutic Recreation.
Standards for the Practice of Therapeutic Recreation.

Professional Credentialing

Members participate in certification through NCTRC (see the section on Certifying and Accrediting Agencies and Academies, page 97). The association has developed a code of ethics.

▍ *Canadian Therapeutic Recreation Association (CTRA)* ▍

Address

7140C Fairmount Drive SE
Calgary, AB, Canada T2H 0X4
phone: (none available)
fax: 514-734-2725
e-mail: ctra@canadian-tr.org
www.canadian-tr.org

History

1996—Association incorporated.

Mission and Goals

The association advocates for the therapeutic recreation profession and its membership by undertaking the following:

• Promoting and facilitating communication between and among members in therapeutic recreation

- Developing and implementing a plan that will lead to national certification of therapeutic recreation practitioners
- Promoting and advocating public awareness and understanding of therapeutic recreation
- Developing and promoting the adoption and implementation of professional standards for the delivery of therapeutic recreation services
- Supporting excellence and advancement in education and research in therapeutic recreation

Publications

The TRibune: Published quarterly.

Professional Credentialing

A special task force is developing a national certification system in Canada.

National Association of Activity Professionals (NAAP)

Address

P.O. Box 5530
Seviervielle, TN 37864
phone: 865-429-0717
fax: 865-453-9914
e-mail: info@thenaap.com
www.thenaap.com

History

1981—Association established.

Mission and Goals

NAAP represents activity professionals in geriatric settings, serves as a catalyst for professional and personal growth, and is recognized by government officials as the voice of the activity profession on national issues concerning long-term-care facilities, retirement living, assisted living, adult day services, and senior-citizen centers.

Publications

NAAP News: A newsletter containing professional development information and updates on government policy affecting long-term care, published six times a year.

Professional Credentialing

Members participate in National Certification Council for Activity Professionals (NCCAP). See the section on Certifying and Accrediting Agencies and Academies, page 97.

International Federation of Adapted Physical Activity (IFAPA)

Address

Dr. Claudine Sherrill
IFAPA Center
11168 Windjammer Dr.
Frisco, TX 75034
phone and fax: (none available)
e-mail: info@ifapa.net
www.ifapa.net

History

1973—Federation founded in Quebec.

Mission and Goals

The federation's purpose is to promote original research, both fundamental and applied, and to encourage the study and application of programs in adapted physical activity for individuals across the life span.

Structural Organization

The organization is divided into seven regions: Africa, Asia, Europe, Middle East, North America, Oceania, and South and Central America.

Services and Programs

The organization's primary service is a biannual international conference. Regional federations hold biannual conferences on alternate years.

Publications

Adapted Physical Activity Quarterly (APAQ).

American College of Sports Medicine (ACSM)

Address

401 W. Michigan St.
Indianapolis, IN 46202-3233
or
P.O. Box 1440
Indianapolis, IN 46206-1440
phone: 317-637-9200
fax: 317-634-7817
e-mail: publicinfo@acsm.org
(see Web site for e-mail addresses for various services)
rwilliams@acsm.org (membership)
www.acsm.org

History

1954—Organization founded (originally called Federation of Sports Medicine).

1975—Exercise Program Directors' Certification, first of the certifications, developed.

Mission and Goals

ACSM advances and integrates scientific research to provide educational and practical applications of exercise science and sports medicine to maintain and enhance physical performance, fitness, health, and quality of life.

Structural Organization

The organization consists of three main categories or areas of interest:

- Basic and applied science
- Education and allied health
- Medicine

The ACSM Foundation was established to receive funds for research and other projects.

Publications

Medicine & Science in Sports & Exercise: First published in 1969.

Professional Credentialing

ACSM has three certification programs: Health and Fitness Instructor, Exercise Specialist, and Clinical Exercise Physiologist. The organization has developed a code of ethics.

International Health, Racquet & Sportsclub Association (IHRSA)

Address

263 Summer St.
Boston, MA 02210
phone: 617-951-0055 or 800-228-4772
fax: 617-951-0056
e-mail: info@ihrsa.org
www.ihrsa.org

History

1981—International Racquet and Sports Association (IRSA) formed as a non-profit trade association.

1991—The National Court Club Association (NCCA) and the National Tennis Association (NTA) merged and joined IRSA and adopted the name International Health, Racquet & Sportsclub Association.

Mission and Goals

IHRSA's purpose is to promote racket sports, fitness, and athletic clubs including businesses that operate racket sports facilities in the United States and throughout the world. The association also strives to perform all acts necessary or incidental to fulfilling its mission.

The association's mission is to grow, protect, and promote the industry and to provide its members with benefits that will help them be more successful.

IHRSA has expanded its leadership role in the fitness industry and endeavors to heighten awareness of the benefits of exercise and membership in IHRSA clubs.

Publications

Club Business International (CBI) Magazine: Published monthly. Membership is open to clubs, not individuals; however, subscription to the magazine is available to individuals and nonmembers.

Professional Credentialing

The organization has developed a code of conduct and membership pledge for club members.

CERTIFYING AND ACCREDITING AGENCIES AND ACADEMIES

This category includes three types of professional organizations: (a) organizations that certify an individual's professional competence, (b) organizations that accredit programs and agencies based on their operational practices, and (c) academies that honor professionals for their contributions to the professional field.

Certification

For professionals, certification is a job credential that communicates to both employers and clients that specific training has been completed and has been recognized by certificate through a sponsoring agency. Professional organizations can use certification to promote professional training and development by requiring individuals to achieve basic certification requirements and to engage in continuing education to retain their certification. However, it's important to note that a certificate is only evidence of having satisfactorily completed certain requirements; it does not guarantee that the certified individual will act on the job in a certain manner. For further discussion of certification, see the December 2002 issue of *Fitness Management.*

Many organizations have formalized their professional development into certification programs. (See Professional Credentialing in the organization descriptions in the preceding categories.) However, for health, fitness, and welfare certifications, it's important to check whether the certifying agency has been approved or accredited by the National Commission for Certifying Agencies (NCCA), the accrediting body of the National Organization for Competency Assurance (NOCA). See www.noca.org/ncca for approved certifications. As of 2004, National Council for Therapeutic Recreation Certification (NCTRC), NATA, and NSCA are approved. For NCCA approval five standards are related to (a) purpose, governance, and resources, (b) responsibilities to stakeholders, (c) assessment instruments, (d) recertification, and (e) maintaining accreditation with NCCA.

In this section only three certifications, which may be termed *overall professional certifications,* are set forth:

CPRP: Certified Park and Recreation Professional

CTRS: Certified Therapeutic Recreation Specialist

CAP: Certified Activity Professional

Information listed includes address, history, administration, criteria for certification, and recertification.

| *Certified Park and Recreation Professional (CPRP)* |

CPRP, formerly called Certified Leisure Professional (CLP), is offered by the National Recreation and Park Association (NRPA) and its state affiliates. (See the section on Recreation, page 46, for a description of NRPA as an organization.)

Address

c/o NRPA
22377 Belmont Ridge Rd.
Ashburn, VA 20148
phone: 703-858-0784
fax: 703-858-0794
e-mail: info@nrpa.org
www.nrpa.org (select Training & Development, then choose Certification)

History

1981—The National Certification Plan was instituted.

1990—Written exam requirement was introduced.

Administration

The National Certification Program is under the general administration of NRPA's National Certification Board (NCB). Members of the board are appointed by NRPA for a specified term. Administration is decentralized to the state affiliates, each of which has a State Professional Certification Board. Contact your state affiliate office (see www.nrpa.org) for specific details for application. Direct national certification is available if you are employed by the military or federal government or live in Alaska, California, Hawaii, Minnesota, Montana, Nevada, North Carolina, Texas, or Washington, DC.

The following outlines the purpose of the national certification plan:

- Establish national standards for certification in the recreation, park resources, and leisure services profession
- Recognize individuals who have qualified
- Guarantee employers that certified personnel have attained stated education and experience qualifications

Criteria for Certification

Criteria are based on a combination of education, experience, and successful completion of an exam. Three alternatives for achieving certification are as follows:

- A bachelor's degree from a National Recreation and Park Association (NRPA) or American Association for Physical Activity and Recreation (AAPAR—formerly AALR) accredited program and successful completion of the CPRP exam.
- A bachelor's degree or higher from a regionally accredited educational institution—without NRPA or AAPAR (formerly AALR) accreditation—with a major in recreation, park resources, and leisure services and two years of full-time experience in a recreation, park resources, and leisure services position following the degree, and successful completion of the CPRP exam.
- A bachelor's degree or higher from a regionally accredited educational institution with a major other than recreation, park resources, and leisure services

and no less than five years of full-time experience following the degree in a recreation, park resources, and leisure services position and successful completion of the CPRP exam.

The exam is designed to assess the base knowledge of job-related tasks common to entry-level professionals. National job analyses were conducted in 1989 and in 1999 to identify the important core competencies of the profession. NRPA's NCB has contracted with Applied Measurements Professionals, Inc. (AMP) to assist with implementation.

Recertification

In order to earn recertification, a person must obtain and verify two continuing education units (CEU) every two years. CEUs are available at the National Congress, state conferences, workshops, and other approved educational programs. One CEU is earned for each 10 hours of education; therefore, a person receives .1 CEU per one-hour session.

Certified Therapeutic Recreation Specialist (CTRS)

CTRS is offered by the National Council for Therapeutic Recreation Certification (NCTRC), which is an independent credentialing organization for therapeutic recreation and recreation therapy.

Address

c/o NCTRC
7 Elmwood Dr.
New City, NY 10956
phone: 845-639-1439
fax: 845-639-1471
e-mail: nctrc@nctrc.org
www.nctrc.org

History

1956—Commission for the Advancement of Hospital Recreation (CAHR) was established with first registration in 1959.

1967—NTRS Registration Board (forerunner to NCTRC) was formed and continued voluntary registration.

1981—NCTRC was organized as an independent council to develop, implement, and administer the therapeutic recreation certification program.

1990—Exam first offered.

1993—Certification program accredited by National Organization for Competency Assurance's (NOCA) National Commission for Certifying Agencies (NCCA).

Administration

The council is composed of a nine-member board of directors, including a consumer and an employer representative, elected by actively certified professionals. The mission of the council is to protect consumers of therapeutic recreation services by promoting quality services by NCTRC certificants. To achieve this mission CTRS undertakes the following:

- Develops standards for certification
- Establishes standards of conduct and applies a disciplinary process
- Conducts entry, recertification, and reentry testing
- Maintains an up-to-date job analysis
- Acts as a liaison with professional organizations regarding standards of practice
- Verifies certification for employers
- Conducts research and development
- Provides recertification and reentry
- Acts as a liaison with educators to provide information and develop opportunities for students to gain the education and experience necessary for certification
- Provides information to the public regarding standards, disciplinary processes, and certification

Criteria for Certification

Two paths lead to certification:

- The academic path requires graduating with a major or option in therapeutic recreation that meets the designated educational requirements, including field experience, and passing the examination.
- The equivalency path consists of five years of full-time work in therapeutic recreation or one year under the supervision of a CTRS and passing the exam.

The exam has been offered since 1990 and is based on a job analysis study. Since 1987 NCTRC has contracted with the Educational Testing Service (ETS) to develop the exam and with the Chauncey Group, a subsidiary of ETS, to administer it.

Recertification

Recertification is required every five years; however, each year of the five, an annual renewal fee and signed renewal or verification form must be submitted. There are two options for recertification:

- Completing a minimum of 480 hours of professional experience and a minimum of 50 hours of continuing education
- Retaking the exam with a passing score

Certified Activity Professional (CAP)

This certification is offered by the National Association of Activity Professionals (NAAP). See the section on Therapeutic Recreation, Disabilities, and Fitness, page 90, for a description of the organization.

Address

c/o NAAP
P.O. Box 62589
Virginia Beach, VA 23466
phone: 757-552-0653
fax: 757-552-0491
e-mail: info@nccap.org
www.nccap.org

History

1986—Certification council established by NAAP.

Administration

The certification program is administered by the National Certification Council for Activity Professionals (NCCAP), which has a board of directors elected by certified members. State representatives provide a local liaison. NCCAP is a credentialing body. It sets standards and criteria to ensure that those served by activity professionals have optimal life experiences.

Criteria for Certification

The four levels of certified activity professionals are as follows:

- Activity assistant certified (AAC)
- Activity director certified (ADC)
- Activity director provisionally certified (ADPC)
- Activity consultant certified (ACC)

Although each level takes a different track to obtaining certification, all must satisfy, at minimum, three qualifying components:

- Academic education: bachelor's degree
- Activity experience: work with elderly populations within the past five years; some volunteer work may be applied
- Continuing education: must have been completed within previous five years

All certified professionals are expected to adhere to a code of ethics and standards of practice in seven areas.

Recertification

Renewal is required every two years. During these two years a person must acquire continuing education hours. An activity assistant requires 20 hours. An activity director and provisionally certified activity director require 30 hours, and an activity consultant requires 40 hours.

Accreditation

Accreditation is one of the marks of a profession (see page 2 in part I). Accreditation is for a program or agency that meets certain standards. Standards are desirable practices for administering or managing an operation, as set forth by the profession. See van der Smissen (2004) for further discussion.

The recreation and park field has four principal accreditation systems:

- Academic curriculum
- Recreation and park agencies
- Organized camps
- Adventure and challenge programs

In addition, related to parks and recreation, there are three other accreditations available. Zoos and aquaria can be accredited (see listing for AZA on page 65). The Council for Standards in Human Services Education (CSHSE) serves human service education (see www.cshse.org). The Commission on Accreditation of Rehabilitation Facilities (CARF) serves rehabilitation and human services programs and facilities (see www.carf.org).

There are four commonalities among accreditation systems:

1. Standards (the basis of all accreditation systems). The standards for the various accreditation systems were developed in some way by professionals in the field and are updated periodically. The agency seeking accreditation may be required to meet a certain percentage of the standards and may be mandated to meet designated standards. There are three parts to each standard:

   a. The standard itself

   b. Interpretation of the standard—to help agencies seeking accreditation to better understand the intent of the standard

   c. Evidence or demonstration of compliance

2. Self-assessment. One of the greatest values of accreditation is in the required self-assessment.

3. Visitation team. After the self-assessment, a team of peers (professionals in the field) visit the agency to verify compliance. The members of the visitation team usually have had special training on interpretation of the standards and how to verify compliance. The team does not determine whether an agency is accredited or not, but reports its compliance findings to a council, commission, or board.

4. Council, commission, or board. This is the entity that reviews the agency's self-assessment and the visitation team's compliance report. The council, commission, or board often has a hearing at which it can ask questions of the agency seeking accreditation and then determines whether or not the agency is to be accredited.

| *Academic Curriculum* |

Academic curriculum accreditation is offered jointly by AAPAR (formerly AALR) and NRPA through the Council on Accreditation (COA).

Address

c/o NRPA
22377 Belmont Ridge Rd.
Ashburn, VA 20148
phone: 703-858-0784
fax: 703-858-0794
e-mail: info@nrpa.org
www.nrpa.org (select Training & Development, then choose Accreditation)

History

1962-74—Standards and evaluative criteria, policies and procedures, and pilot testing were developed. This was initiated by the Professional Development Committee of the American Recreation Society (ARS).

1970—NRPA Board of Trustees established a Board of Professional Education.

1974—Council on Accreditation was established jointly by NRPA (ARS merged into the NRPA in 1966) and AALR.

1975—Council officially adopted and published *Standards and Evaluative Criteria* as document to be used for accreditation.

1986—Commission on Postsecondary Accreditation (COPA), now the Council for Higher Education Accreditation (CHEA), recognized the council.

1990—Major revision of standards with a conceptual framework to provide greater flexibility for specialized programs.

2004—Another major revision of the standards.

See *Historical Perspectives on the Development of the NRPA/AALR Council on Accreditation* edited by Barbara A. Hawkins.

Administration

The Council on Accreditation (COA) administers the program. The council is composed of 10 members appointed by the two sponsoring organizations, AAPAR (formerly AALR) and NRPA, and includes educators, practitioners, and a public representative. The council is recognized by the Council for Higher Education Accreditation (CHEA) (www.chea.org), successor to COPA, and is a member of the Association of Specialized & Professional Accreditors (ASPA) (www.aspa-usa.org).

The purpose of the council is to assure program quality and to assist in program improvement.

Criteria for Accreditation

COA accredits four-year baccalaureate programs in colleges and universities for professional preparation for entry-level positions in recreation and park. The standards are descriptive statements of quality concerning the organization and operation of the academic program. However, institutional accreditation cannot guarantee the quality of graduates or individual courses. The standards are divided into several sections:

- Organization and operation standards. These include characteristics of the academic unit, faculty, philosophy and goals, students, administration, and instructional resources.
- Program content standards. These include foundation understandings and professional competencies.
- Foundation understandings. These are equivalent to a university's general education requirements.
- Professional competencies. These include conceptual foundations assessment, planning and evaluation, leisure services profession, legislative and legal aspects, leisure services delivery systems, field experiences, programming strategies, administration, and management.
- Options. While the previous standards provide the basic program, an institution may seek accreditation of specialized areas by adding in-depth academic work designated by the standards. The four areas in which options are offered are leisure services management, natural resources recreation management, leisure and recreation program delivery, and therapeutic recreation.

Reaccreditation

A program is accredited for five years. To earn reaccreditation, the program must meet the original standards.

❙ *Recreation and Park Agencies* ❙

Agencies that provides park, recreation, and leisure services, not just public recreation and park agencies can be accredited. The National Recreation and Park Association (NRPA) provides logistical support and sponsors the accreditation program with the American Academy for Park and Recreation Administration (AAPRA). The program is administered by the Commission for Accreditation of Park and Recreation Agencies (CAPRA).

Address

c/o NRPA
22377 Belmont Ridge Rd.
Ashburn, VA 20148
phone: 703-858-0784
fax: 703-858-0794
e-mail: info@nrpa.org
www.nrpa.org (select Training & Development, then choose Agency Accreditation)

History

1965—National Recreation Association published *Standards and Evaluative Criteria*, and revised it in 1972.

1989—National committee formed by AAPRA, then joined by NRPA.

1989-1993—Standards and procedures were developed, a pilot program on training the visitors was conducted, and the committee recommended the final version of the st`andards and procedures.

1993—Commission replaced the committee, formally adopted the accreditation program and its standards and procedures, and became fully responsible for administering the program.

1999—Military version of standards were adopted and first installation accredited in 2003.

Administration

The accreditation program is administered by CAPRA, an independent body that is sanctioned by NRPA and AAPRA. The commission is composed of 13 members, four selected by NRPA, four by the academy, and five by AAPAR (formerly AALR), International City Management Association (ICMA), Council of Executive Directors of the NRPA (CED), National Association of Counties (NACo), and Armed Forces Recreation Society (AFRS), a branch of NRPA.

Criteria for Accreditation

Designated fundamental standards (36) must be met and 85 percent of the remainder. Standards are separated into the following 10 categories:

* Agency authority, role, and responsibility: legal authority and jurisdiction, mission, goals and objectives, policy formulation and review, and relationships
* Planning: trends analysis, community planning, strategic planning, and comprehensive planning
* Organization and administration: organization, administrative facilities, public information, community relations, marketing, management information systems, communications, planning, and research

- Human resources: employees, volunteers, consultants, and contract employees
- Finance: fiscal policy, fiscal management, auditing and accountability, and budgeting procedures
- Program and services management: programs and services determinants, nature of services and program delivery, objectives, outreach, scope of program opportunities, selection of program content, types of participants, education for leisure, and program evaluation
- Facility and land use management: acquisition, development, encroachment, disposal, maintenance and operations, facilities management, fleets, agency-owned equipment, natural resource management, maintenance personnel, depreciation, and replacement
- Security and public safety: authority, traffic control, law enforcement, and general security
- Risk management: policy, risk manager, plan, risk analysis and control approaches, employee involvement, operational procedures, and risk accounting
- Evaluation and research: systematic evaluation program, demonstration projects and action research, evaluation personnel, and employee education

The commission sponsored a manual of 21 chapters and more than 600 pages, *Management of Park and Recreation Agencies,* edited by Betty van der Smissen and others, based on these standards. The second edition was published in 2005 with a compendium of field examples. It is available through NRPA.

Reaccreditation

Accreditation is good for five years; however, at the end of five years the reaccreditation review is limited to standards with which the agency was not in compliance on the initial review and with randomly selected additional standards in each category. An on-site visit is required. At the end of 10 years, a full-scale self-assessment and review is required.

▌ *Organized Camps* ▌

The American Camping Association (ACA) accredits organized camping programs. A camp is defined as (a) a sustained experience of at least five days, (b) group living that includes planned and organized group interaction that provides personal development and instructional opportunities, and (c) taking place outdoors with the natural environment as a principal setting. Accreditation is available for camps operating programs and services on one's own property or on property belonging to someone else. ACA also offers accreditation for conference and retreat centers.

Address

5000 State Rd. 67 N
Martinsville, IN 46151-7902
phone: 765-342-8456
fax: 765-342-2065
e-mail: (see Web site for e-mail addresses for specific departments and topics)
www.acacamps.org

History

1940—ACA began assembling and developing a set of standards that represented a consensus of the organized camping movement.

1948—First standards were officially adopted.

1956—Day camp standards were first adopted.

1961—Travel and family camp standards were adopted.

1968—Major research study conducted to improve the standards.

1972—Revisions recommended from the research approved.

1974—Standards for people with physical disabilities were adopted, in cooperation with the National Easter Seal Society (NESS).

1980—Standards for people with mental retardation were adopted with input from state associations for people with mental retardation.

1982—Standards for camps serving people with diabetes were adopted with input from the American Diabetes Association (ADA).

1984—All standards previously adopted, for camp accreditation and site approval, were consolidated.

1990—Standards were divided into two parts: those focusing on health and safety issues became the basic standards document, and those reflecting good business practices were placed in a separate self-assessment document.

1992—Standards were revised slightly to reflect concerns of the Americans with Disabilities Act of 1990 (ADA).

1993—Standards for conference and retreat center operations were adopted.

1998—Standards were revised and restructured, combining the previous camp accreditation and site approval standards into one document.

2004—National Standards Commission (NCS) began another major structural revision; check its Web site for updates.

Administration

ACA's National Standards Commission (formerly Board) administers the accreditation program through the ACA's chartered sections, each of which has a standards committee. The National Standards Commission is composed of up to 12 members with the following criteria:

- At least 1/3 camp directors, 1/3 standards chairs, and up to 1/3 specialized expertise
- Each of the five regions must be represented
- Consideration given to diversity of types of agencies and camps

Members are appointed for four-year rotating terms by the National Standards Chair, who is appointed by the National ACA President for a three-year term. The purpose of accreditation is as follows:

- Educate camp owners and directors in the key aspects of camp operation, particularly program quality and the health and safety of campers and staff
- Assist the public in selecting camps that meet industry-accepted and government-recognized standards

Criteria for Accreditation

Standards are applicable to all types of programs including day and resident, trip and travel, therapeutic, all types of sponsoring organizations, independently owned, religiously affiliated, city or county, and nonprofit organizations. However, certain standards are applicable only to day camps, resident camps, short-term residential programs, and rental or camps that rent to user groups.

A camp must comply with 80 percent of the standards in each applicable section. Some of the standards are mandatory. The standards are separated into 10 sections (the number of mandatory standards in each section are listed in parentheses):

- Site and food service: 32 standards (2)
- Transportation: 19 standards (1)
- Health and wellness: 23 standards (2)
- Operational management: 21 standards (1)
- Human resources: 21 standards (0)
- Program design and activities: 24 standards (1)
- Program, aquatics, with subcategories of swimming and boating: 35 standards (9)
- Program, adventure challenge: 16 standards (0)
- Program, horseback riding: 13 standards (0)
- Program, trip and travel: 20 standards (2)

In addition to these standards, a self-assessment entitled Additional Professional Practices is used in conjunction with and as a complement to the accreditation standards, but it is not scored as part of the standards compliance. Thirty-nine practices are distributed among the standards sections: site and food service (14), operational management (10), human resources (5), and program design and activities (10).

Reaccreditation

Accreditation is valid for three years. After three years, the camp is revisited to verify compliance with the standards.

▌ *Adventure and Challenge Programs* ▌

The Association for Experiential Education (AEE)—through its council on accreditation—accredits adventure and challenge programs that have explicit educational or therapeutic program objectives or both and programs in which participants' growth and development are major program objectives and in which participants have a sense of control over what they are doing and the systems and equipment they are using.

Address

3775 Iris, Ste.4
Boulder, CO 80301-2043
phone: 303-440-8844
fax: 303-440-9581
e-mail: accreditation@aee.org
www.aee.org

History

Prior—Had a system of peer review and published best practices.

1989—Task force created to develop accreditation program.

1994—Council on Accreditation Standards for Adventure Programs (CASAP) officially established.

Administration

The AEE Board of Directors appoints a 15-member council to administer the program.

Criteria for Certification

To earn certification a program must meet all applicable standards, which are divided into five chapters. All programs must meet the general standards in chapters 1 and 2, plus those activity-oriented standards in chapters 3 through 5 that apply to the program. While the program is expected to meet all applicable standards, the council may use its judgment in a situation that indicates a deviation from the standard, as evidenced by the site review team. The five chapters are as follows:

- Chapter 1 Philosophical, Ethical, and Educational Concerns: philosophy, education, and program ethics
- Chapter 2 Risk Management: program management and operations, staff qualifications, transportation, equipment, nutrition and hygiene, program and activity planning, environment and culture, and international considerations
- Chapter 3 Technical Skills, Land Activities: hiking and backpacking, camping, running, initiative games and problem-solving exercises, high- and low-challenge courses, orienteering, bicycle touring, mountain biking, artificial-wall climbing, bouldering, top-rope rock climbing, rappelling, lead climbing, multipitch climbing, mountaineering, glacier travel, snow and ice climbing, caving, river crossing, snowshoeing, cross country and back-country skiing, solos, horseback riding and pack animals, service projects, and expeditions and remote wilderness travel
- Chapter 4 Technical Skills, Water Activities: personal flotation devices, flat-water canoeing and kayaking, white-water canoeing and kayaking, river rafting, sea kayaking, sailing, snorkeling, and scuba diving
- Chapter 5 Technical Skills, Air Activities: parapet, hang gliding, and parachuting

Reaccreditation

Reaccreditation is required after the initial three-year accreditation and every five years thereafter. A report must be filed annually.

Academies

Academies are honorary organizations. Academy members, in accordance with specified criteria, elect professionals to the academy to recognize their accomplishments in a particular field of the profession. Academies are valuable to students because they identify the profession's leaders (see the section on Leadership in part I, page 16). Academies usually have a limited service program; however, some give student awards (see each academy's Web site).

The recreation and park field honors members through four principal academies:

AAPRA: American Academy for Park and Recreation Administration

ALA: American Leisure Academy

ALS: Academy of Leisure Sciences

NAS: North American Society of Health, Physical Education, Recreation, Sport, and Dance Professionals

▎ *American Academy for Park and Recreation Administration (AAPRA)* ▎

Address

P.O. Box 1040
Mahomet, IL 61853
phone: 217-586-3360
fax: 217-586-5724
e-mail: jcpotts@ccfpd.com
www.rpts.tamu.edu/aapra

History

1980—Formed as an organization of distinguished practitioners and scholars committed to advancing the recreation and park field.

Mission and Goals

The mission of AAPRA is to advance knowledge related to the administration of recreation and parks, encourage scholarly efforts by practitioners and educators that will enhance the practice of recreation and park administration, promote broader public understanding of the importance of recreation and park to the public good, and conduct research, publish scholarly papers, and sponsor seminars related to the advancement of recreation and park administration.

Membership

Membership in the academy is limited to 125 practicing professionals, of whom no more than 25 percent may be educators. To be eligible, a person must (a) serve no less than 15 years in a high level of administration in a recreation and park agency or an institution of higher education, (b) demonstrate leadership, and (c) have a desire to contribute to the advancement of recreation and park through participation in the affairs of the academy. (See Web site for membership roster.)

Selected Functions

- *Journal of Park and Recreation Administration*
- AAPRA and NRPA jointly sponsor the Commission for Accreditation of Park and Recreation Agencies (CAPRA) (see previous section on Accreditation)

▎ *American Leisure Academy (ALA)* ▎

Address

c/o AALR
1900 Association Dr.
Reston, VA 20191
phone: 703-476-3472
fax: 703-476-9527
e-mail: aalr@aahperd.org
www.aahperd.org (search for ALA)

History

1997—Founded by the American Association for Leisure and Recreation (AALR).

Mission and Goals

ALA serves as a forum to promote and advance the quality of life of Americans through creative and meaningful leisure and recreation experience. The following are its objectives:

- Advance knowledge related to leisure and leisure services
- Serve as a forum for networking and exchange of ideas related to leisure
- Recognize and acknowledge the contributions of professional educators, practitioners, and others credited with advancing leisure and recreation concepts and ideas
- Provide advice and counsel to the officers and elected board members of the American Association for Leisure and Recreation

Membership

Membership is limited to 50 individuals; election requires a two-thirds vote. Membership is divided into four categories. Their eligibility criteria are listed.

- Senior fellows: (a) 20 or more years of experience as an educator or practicing professional, (b) previously served as an officer of AALR or served as a J.B. Nash Scholar, (c) recognized as an outstanding scholar in the recreation and leisure service field, and (d) committed to advancing the goals and ideals of the recreation and leisure service movement
- Fellows: (a) 20 or more years experience as an educator or practitioner, (b) recognized as an outstanding scholar in the recreation and leisure service field or acknowledged for contributions to the profession on an international basis, and (c) committed to advancing the goals and ideals of the recreation and leisure service movement
- International fellows: recognized for their contributions to the leisure movement throughout the world
- Emeritus fellows: retired from regular employment and previously elected as a senior fellow or fellow

See the organization's Web site for a membership roster.

Academy of Leisure Science (ALS)

Address

c/o SPRE
22377 Belmont Ridge Rd.
Ashburn, VA 20148
phone: (703) 858-2150
fax: (703) 858-0794
e-mail: info@nrpal.org
www.academyofleisuresciences.org

History

1980—Established with 30 founding fellows.

Mission and Goals

The central purpose of ALS is to promote the intellectual advancement of leisure sciences. The purpose is carried out in three ways:

- Recognizing outstanding scholars establishes a network among those who have contributed to the intellectual advancement of leisure sciences.
- Holding meetings and other activities establishes forums for exchanging knowledge and ideas advancing the intellectual understanding of leisure.
- The activities of its committees and individual members encourage and promote research and the scholarly study of leisure among those who have demonstrated interest, potential, and competence.

Membership

Individuals are nominated by current members; election requires a two-thirds vote. Criteria include (a) direct engagement in the leisure science profession; (b) demonstrated competence for not less than 10 years, as evidenced by contributions to the scholarly literature of the field in appropriate quality and quantity, recognized leadership and extensive significant participation in professional associations and organizations, and acknowledged outstanding performance as a teacher or leader, administrator, practitioner, or researcher in the field of leisure; (c) willingness to further the goals of the academy and participate actively in its affairs. See the organization's Web site for a membership roster.

North American Society of Health, Physical Education, Recreation, Sport, and Dance Professionals (North American Society of HPERSD Professionals or NAS)

Address

The organization has no specific office or Web site; contact American Alliance for Health, Physical Education, Recreation and Dance (AAHPERD) or Canadian Association for Health, Physical Education, Recreation and Dance (CAHPERD) for information and current officers. (See pages 47 and 50 for contact information for these two organizations.)

History

2000—Founded by AAHPERD and CAHPERD.

Mission and Goals

The purpose of NAS is to recognize outstanding professionals from the allied professions of health education, physical education, recreation, sport, and dance in North America.

Membership

Members are known as fellows. A fellow is a person who resides in North America who has been active in one or more of the recognized disciplines of AAHPERD or CAHPERD. More specifically, individuals must meet the following criteria for membership:

- Hold current membership in AAHPERD or CAHPERD
- Have demonstrated outstanding competence through professional involvement for at least 20 years
- Meet at least two of the following: service as an educator in the public or private sector in any community or educational setting; service in administration in the public or private sector in any community or educational setting; significant contributions to the professional literature in his or her discipline; significant contributions to the scholarly literature in his or her discipline; sustained involvement in leadership activities in his or her discipline; other evidence of leadership in the profession including service to the community at large.

Part IV

Selected Professional Resources

Professional literature is one of the marks of a profession (see part I). The recreation, parks, and leisure services profession has a considerable amount of literature written by professionals and others in related fields. This part of the book provides a basic bibliography of the literature; it does not include activity or how-to books.

The bibliography is divided into 12 functional sections. For the most part, these sections parallel the categories in parts II and III. Some books could have been placed in more than one section, but were not; therefore, it is important to check related sections, too. The 12 sections are:

Foundations of Leisure and Recreation

Includes resources about philosophy, history, sociology, and psychology. Does not include resources about play.

Programming and Leadership

Includes books on leisure education and special events, but does not include resources on youth sports or program activities.

Therapeutic Recreation

Includes resources on recreation for older citizens and people with disabilities. Books on specific programs of therapeutic modalities, such as pets, horticulture, music, drama, and physical activity and health, are not included, nor are the many books on the various disabilities, aging, and youth-at-risk.

Sport Management, Physical Activity, and Fitness

Includes resources on sport management from a leisure and recreation perspective. It does not include resources on sport and fitness activities or on the conduct of scientific research about exercise and physical activity.

Commercial Recreation and Tourism

Includes resources on employee recreation.

Evaluation and Research Methodology and Statistics

Includes resources on action research, focus groups, and needs assessment.

Management and Administration

Includes resources about marketing, finance, and personnel.

Areas, Facilities, and Urban Park Planning

Does not include books on specific facilities such as aquatics and skate parks.

Natural Resource–Based Recreation Management and Policy

Includes outdoor recreation resources.

Outdoor and Environment-Related Programs

Includes resources on interpretation, environmental education, camping, and adventure programs. Resources for sports played outdoors, nature guides, or activities are not included.

Classical

Includes books published before 1990 from nearly all of the functional sections.

Selected Professional and Research Periodicals

Includes both journals and newsletters.

The bibliography is not an exhaustive list, but rather selected resources primarily published since 1990. Each educator and practitioner has his or her own preference, which may not be included in the bibliography. Therefore students should ask them which resources they have found most useful. This bibliography is a basic list of resources only. Students should begin acquiring the books in their area of academic or professional emphasis. Some of these books will be used as texts and required readings in various courses.

Students also should begin acquiring additional resources in their particular career areas. Faculty associated with your particular area of interest can recommend resources for an extended library. Bibliographies in books and articles in professional periodicals also provide additional resources. Students can also consult the extended resource lists used in most courses, which are specific to the focus of the course. These resource lists usually cite periodical articles, agency and association materials, chapters in books, proceedings, monographs, and bulletins. An excellent start point can also be the bibliographies at the end of each of the 21 chapters in *Management of Park and Recreation Agencies* (see page 129 in the section on Management and Administration for the citation). Some professional organizations publish bibliographies, proceedings, and other resource materials (see part III). Many informational resources are available on the Internet, but should not replace the resources included in this bibliography. When using an Internet site, be sure to verify the credibility of the source and information through printed publications or contact sources.

Doctoral students should be familiar with the literature across the entire field, that is, the references listed in all sections. Educational institutional libraries should have all of the books listed in the bibliography, plus more. Agencies and associations should have the books and other resource materials listed in the areas for their programs and services.

Because of the extensive number of books and periodicals available, the books listed here are, for the most part, only those published since 1990. However, just because a book is older does not mean it is not useful. Many books written prior to 1990 still provide excellent resources. A few books are listed in the Classics category, which includes books that represent the various sections. They provide a foundation for professional thought and practice and an understanding of the professional leadership and the evolution of the profession and its various fields. On the other hand, just because a book is new does not mean it is necessarily useful for your particular purpose.

It is essential that you keep up-to-date by being aware of new editions of the books listed and new books published. These can be identified through professional periodicals and publishers' brochures and catalogues and through talking with other professionals and exhibitors at conferences. Some of the professional organizations maintain bookstores.

Generally, books are written by leaders in the field; therefore, to learn more about the people in the field, you should learn about the author's professional activity, contribution to the profession, and where he or she is from.

FOUNDATIONS OF LEISURE AND RECREATION

This section includes philosophy, history, sociology, and psychology resources. Resources about play are not included.

Bammel, G., and L.L. Bammel. 1996. *Leisure and human behavior.* 3rd ed. Dubuque, IA: Brown & Benchmark.

Cordes, K. A., and H.M. Ibrahim. 2003. *Applications in recreation and leisure for today and in the future.* 3rd ed. Boston: WCB/McGraw-Hill.

Cross, G. 1990. *A social history of leisure, since 1960.* State College, PA: Venture Publishing.

Csikszentmihalyi, M. 1990. *Flow, the psychology of optimal experience.* New York: Harpers Perennial.

Csikszentmihalyi, M. 2003. *Good business: Leadership, flow, and the making of meaning.* New York: Penguin Putnam.

Driver, B.L., P.J. Brown, and G.L. Peterson, eds. 1991. *Benefits of leisure.* State College, PA: Venture Publishing.

Dustin, D.L. 1999. *The wilderness within: Reflection on leisure and life.* 2nd ed. Champaign, IL: Sagamore Publishing.

Dustin, D.L., L. McAvoy, and J.H. Schultz. 2002. *Stewards of access/custodians of choice: A philosophical foundation for the park and recreation profession.* 3rd ed. Champaign, IL: Sagamore Publishing.

Edginton, C.R., et al. 2002. *Leisure and life satisfaction: Foundational perspectives.* 3rd ed. New York: McGraw-Hill.

Fain, G.S, ed. 1991. *Leisure and ethics.* Reston, VA: American Alliance for Health, Physical Education, Recreation and Dance.

Florida, R. 2002. *The rise of the creative class, and how it's transforming work, leisure, community and everyday life.* New York: Basic Books.

Freysinger, V.J., and J.R. Kelly. 2004. *21st century leisure: Current issues.* 2nd ed. State College, PA: Venture Publishing.

Godbey, G. 1997. *Leisure and leisure services in the 21st century.* State College, PA: Venture Publishing.

Godbey, G. 2003. *Leisure in your life: An exploration.* 6th ed. State College, PA: Venture Publishing.

Goodale, T.L., and P.A. Witt, eds. 1991. *Recreation and leisure: Issues in an era of change.* 3rd ed. State College, PA: Venture Publishing.

Heintzman, P., G.E. Van Andel, and T.L. Visker, eds. 1994. *Christianity and leisure: Issues in a pluralistic society.* Sioux City, IA: Dordt College Press.

Henderson, K., M.D. Bialeschki, S.M. Shaw, and V. J. Freysinger. 1989. *A leisure of one's own: A feminist perspective on women's leisure.* State College, PA: Venture Publishing.

Henderson K.A., M.D. Bialeschki, S.M. Shaw, and V.J. Freysinger. 1996. *Both gains and gaps: Feminist perspectives on women's leisure.* State College, PA: Venture Publishing.

Henderson K.A. et al. 2001. *Introduction to recreation and leisure services.* 8th ed. State College, PA: Venture Publishing.

Ibrahim, H. 1989. *Pioneers in leisure and recreation.* Reston, VA: American Alliance for Health, Physical Education, Recreation and Dance.

Ibrahim, H. 1991. *Leisure and society: A comparative approach.* Dubuque, IA: Brown.

Jackson, E.L, and T.L. Burton, eds. 1989. *Understanding leisure and recreation: Mapping the past, charting the future.* State College, PA: Venture Publishing.

Jackson, E.L., and T.L. Burton, eds. 1999. *Leisure studies: Prospects for the 21st century.* State College, PA: Venture Publishing.

Jarvie, G., and J. Maguire. 1994. *Sport and leisure in social thought.* New York: Routledge.

Kelly, J.R. 1996. *Leisure.* 3rd ed. Needham Heights, MA: Allyn & Bacon.

Kelly, J.R., and G. Godbey. 1992. *Sociology of leisure.* State College, PA: Venture Publishing.

Kleiber, D. 1999. *Leisure experience and human dimension.* New York: Basic Books.

Kraus, R. 1997. *Recreation and leisure in modern society.* 5th ed. Glenview, IL: Scott Foresman/Little, Brown.

Kraus, R. 2000. *Leisure in a changing America: Trends and issues for the 21st century.* Needham Heights, MA: Allyn & Bacon.

Kraus, R., E. Barber, and I. Shapiro. 2001. *Introduction to leisure services: Career perspectives.* Champaign, IL: Sagamore Publishing.

Leitner, M., S. F. Leitner, and Associates. 1996. *Leisure enhancement.* 2nd ed. New York: Haworth.

Mannell, R.C., and D.A. Kleiber. 1997. *A social psychology of leisure.* State College, PA: Venture Publishing.

Murphy, James F., et al. 1991. *Leisure systems: Critical concepts and applications.* Champaign, IL: Sagamore Publishing.

Robinson, J.P., and G. Godbey. 1997. *Time for life.* University City, PA: Penn State University Press.

Rojek, C. 1995. *Decentring leisure.* Thousand Oaks, CA: Sage Publications.

Ruskin, H., and A. Sivan, eds. 1995. *Leisure education towards the 21st century.* Provo, UT: Brigham Young University.

Russell, R.V. 2002. *Pastimes, the context of contemporary leisure.* 2nd ed. Champaign, IL: Sagamore Publishing.

Schor, J.B. 1992. *The overworked American: The unexpected decline of leisure.* New York: Basic Books.

Searle, M.S., and R.E. Brayley. 2000. *Leisure services in Canada: An introduction.* 2nd ed. State College, PA: Venture Publishing.

Sefton, J.M., and W.K. Mummery. 1995. *Benefits of recreation research update.* State College, PA: Venture Publishing.

Shivers, J.S., and L.J. deLisle. 1997. *The story of leisure: Context, concepts, and current controversy.* Champaign, IL: Human Kinetics.

Stebbins, R.A. 2002. *The organizational basis of leisure participation: A motivational exploration.* State College, PA: Venture Publishing.

Wynne, D. 1998. *Leisure, lifestyle, and the new middle class: A case study.* London: Routledge & Kegan Paul.

PROGRAMMING AND LEADERSHIP

This list includes books on leisure education and special events, but does not include resources on youth sports or program activities. For resources related to diversity, volunteers, and supervision of personnel, see the section on Management and Administration, which begins on page 129. See the section on Evaluation and Research Methodology and Statistics for books on program evaluation (page 125). There are so many books about specific program areas and activities that they're easy to find, so these have not been included.

Allen, L., R. Hardwell, B. Stevens, and K. Paisley. 1998. *Benefits-based programming of recreation services training manual.* Ashburn, VA: National Recreation and Parks Association.

American Sport Education Program (ASEP). 1996. *Event management for sport directors.* Champaign, IL: Human Kinetics.

Bass, B.M. 1990. *Bass and Stogdill's handbook of leadership: Theory, research, and managerial application.* 3rd ed. New York: The Free Press.

Berlonghi, A. 1994. *The special event risk management manual,* Special Event Liability Series, vol. 1. Dana Point, CA: author. P.O. Box 3454, Dana Point, CA, 92629.
Also distributed by Bookmasters in Mansfield, OH.

Berlonghi, A. 1996. *Special event security management, loss prevention, and emergency services,* Special Event Liability Series, vol. 2. Dana Point, CA: author. P.O. Box 3454, Dana Point, CA, 92629.
Also distributed by Bookmasters in Mansfield, OH.

Catherwood, D., and R. Van Kirk. 1992. *The complete guide to special events management.* New York: Wiley.

Chase, C.M., and J.E. Chase. 1996. *Recreation and leisure programming.* Dubuque, IA: Eddie Bowers.

Dattilo, J. 1999. *Leisure education program planning: A systematic approach.* 2nd ed. State College, PA: Venture Publishing.

Dattilo, J. 2000. *Leisure education specific programs.* State College, PA: Venture Publishing.

DeGraaf, D., D. Jordan, and K. DeGraaf. 1999. *Programming for parks, recreation, and leisure services: A servant leadership approach.* State College, PA: Venture Publishing.

Dreeszen, C., and P. Korza, eds. 1998. *Fundamentals of local arts management.* 3rd ed. Amherst, MA: Arts Extension Service, Division of Continuing Education, University of Massachusetts. *In cooperation with the National Assembly of Local Arts Agencies.*

Driver, B.L., P.J. Brown, and G.L. Peterson, eds. 1991. *Benefits of leisure.* State College, PA: Venture Publishing.

Dustin, D., L. McAvoy, and J. Schultz. 2002. *Stewards of access/custodians of choice.* 3rd ed. Champaign, IL: Sagamore Publishing.

Eccles, J., and J.A. Gootman, eds. 2002. *Community programs to provide youth development.* Washington, DC: National Academy Press.

Edginton, C.R., S.D. Hudson, R.B. Dieser, and S.R. Edginton. 2004. *Leisure programming: A service centered and benefits approach.* 4th ed. Boston: WCB/McGraw-Hill.

Edginton, C.R., S.D. Hudson, and K.G. Scholl. 2005. *Leadership for recreation and leisure programs and settings.* 3rd ed. Champaign, IL: Sagamore Publishing.

Edginton S.R., and C.R. Edginton. 1994. *Youth programs, promoting quality service.* Champaign, IL: Sagamore Publishing.

Edginton, C.R., C.L. Kowalski, and S.W. Randall. 2005. *Youth work: Emerging perspectives in youth development.* Champaign, IL: Sagamore Publishing.

Farrell, P., and H.M. Lundegren. 1991. *The process of recreation programming.* 3rd ed. State College, PA: Venture Publishing.

Fisher, J.C., and K.M. Cole. 1993. *Leadership and management of volunteer programs.* San Francisco: Jossey-Bass.

Florida, R. 2002. *The rise of the creative class.* New York: Basic Books.

Foley, J., and V. Ward. 1998. *Urban recreation: Human development and human potential.* Champaign, IL: Sagamore Publishing.

Hart, C.H., ed. 1993. *Children on playgrounds: Research perspectives and applications.* Albany, NY: State University of New York Press.

Jackson, R. 1997. *Making special events fit in the 21st century.* Champaign, IL: Sagamore Publishing.

Jordan, D.J. 2001. *Leadership in leisure services: Making a difference.* 2nd ed. State College, PA: Venture Publishing.

Kettner, P.M., R.M. Moroney, and L.L. Martin. 1990. *Designing and managing programs: An effectiveness-based approach.* Newbury Park, CA: Sage Publications.

Klopovic, J., M.L. Vasu, and D.L. Yearwood. 2003. *Effective program practices for at-risk youth: A continuum of community-based programs.* Kingston, NJ: Civic Research Institute.

Kraus, R. 1997. *Recreation programming: A benefits-driven approach.* Boston: Allyn & Bacon.

McLaughlin, M.W., M.A. Irby, and J. Langman. 1994. *Urban sanctuaries: Neighborhood organizations in the lives and futures of inner-city youth.* San Francisco: Jossey-Bass.

Moon, M.S., ed. 1994. *Making school and community recreation fun for everyone: Places and ways to integrate.* Baltimore: Paul H. Brookes Publishing.

Mundy, J. 1998. *Leisure education, theory and practice.* 2nd ed. Champaign, IL: Sagamore Publishing.

National Recreation and Park Association (NRPA). 1994. *Beyond "fun and games": Emerging roles of public recreation.* Arlington, VA: National Recreation and Park Association.

Prosser, A., and A. Rutledge. 2003. *Special events and festivals: How to plan, organize and implement.* State College, PA: Venture Publishing.

Rojek, C. 2000. *Leisure and culture.* New York: St. Martin's Press.

Rossman, J.R., and B.E. Schlatter. 2003. *Recreation programming: Designing leisure experiences.* 4th ed. Champaign, IL: Sagamore Publishing.

Ruskin, H., and A. Sivan, eds. 1995. *Leisure education: Towards the 21st century.* Provo, UT: Brigham Young University.

Sample, S.B. 2002. *The contrarian's guide to leadership.* San Francisco: Jossy-Bass.

Schmader, S.W., and R. Jackson. 1997. *Special events: Inside and out.* 2nd ed. Champaign, IL: Sagamore Publishing.

Spergel, I.A. 1995. *The youth gang problem: A community approach.* New York: Oxford Press.

Stanley, A. 2003. *The next generation leader.* Sisters, OR: Multnomah Publishers.

Stebbins, R.A. and M. Graham, eds. 2004. *Volunteering as leisure/leisure as volunteering.* Cambridge, MA: CABI Publishing.

Thorne, B. 1993. *Gender play: Girls and boys in school.* New Brunswick, NJ: Rutgers University Press.

Witkin, B.R., and J.W. Altschuld. 1995. *Planning and conducting needs assessments: A practical guide.* Thousand Oaks, CA: Sage Publications.

Witt, P.A., and J.L. Crompton, eds. 1999. *Public recreation in high risk environments: Programs that work* (updated). Ashburn, VA: National Recreation and Park Association.

THERAPEUTIC RECREATION

This list includes resources on recreation for older citizens and people with disabilities. Books on specific programs of therapeutic modalities, such as pets, horticulture, music, drama, and physical activity and health, are not included, nor are the many books on the various disabilities, aging, and youth-at-risk. For resources on sport for people with disabilities and for senior citizens, see page 120 in the section on Sport Management, Physical Activity, and Fitness. Also check the section on Outdoor and Environment-Related Programs, page 135.

Anderson, L., and C. Brown Kress. 2003. *Inclusion: Including people with disabilities in parks and recreation opportunities.* State College, PA: Venture Publishing.

Austin, D.R. 2004. *Therapeutic recreation: Processes and techniques.* 5th ed. Champaign, IL: Sagamore Publishing.

Avery, L.F. 1997. *Activity programming in long-term care.* New York: Springer Publishing.

Baglin, C.A., M.E.B. Lewis, and B. Williams. 2004. *Recreation and leisure for persons with emotional problems and challenging behaviors.* Champaign, IL: Sagamore Publishing.

Brannan, S., et al. 2003. *Including youth with disabilities in outdoor programs: Best practices, outcomes, and resources.* Champaign, IL: Sagamore Publishing.

Brasile, F., T.K. Skalko, and J. Burlingame, eds. 1998. *Perspectives in recreation therapy: Issues of a dynamic profession.* Ravensdale, WA: Idyll Arbor.

Buettner, L., and S.L. Martin. 1995. *Therapeutic recreation in the nursing home.* State College, PA: Venture Publishing.

Bullock, C.C., and M.J. Mahon. 2001. *Introduction to recreation services for people with disablilities.* 2nd ed. Champaign, IL: Sagamore Publishing.

Carter, M.J., and S. LeConey. 2004. *Therapeutic recreation programs in the community.* Champaign, IL: Sagamore Publishing.

Carter, M.J., G.E. Van Andel, and G.M. Robb. 2003. *Therapeutic recreation: A practical approach.* 3rd ed. Prospects Heights, IL: Waveland Press.

Cohen, M.J. 1997. *Reconnecting with nature.* Corvallis, OR: Ecopress.

Compton, D.M., ed. 1997. *Issues in therapeutic recreation: Toward the new millennium.* 2nd ed. Champaign, IL: Sagamore Publishing.

Coyle, C.P., et al., eds. 1991. *Benefits of therapeutic recreation: A consensus view.* Ravensdale, WA: Idyll Arbor.

Dattilo, J. 2000. *Facilitation techniques in therapeutic recreation.* State College, PA: Venture Publishing.

Dattilo, J. 2002. *Inclusive leisure services: Responding to the rights of people with disabilities.* 2nd ed. State College, PA: Venture Publishing.

DePauw, K., and S.P. Gavron. 2004. *Disability and sport.* 2nd ed. Champaign, IL: Human Kinetics.

Doll-Tepper, G., M. Kroner, and W. Sonnenshein, eds. 2001. *New horizons in sport for athletes with a disability,* vol. 1. Oxford, UK: Meyer & Meyer Sport. *Proceedings of the International VISTA '99 Conference.*

Eichstaedt, C.B., and B.W. Lavay. 1992. *Physical activity for individuals with mental retardation, infancy through adulthood.* Champaign, IL: Human Kinetics.

Gething, L. 1997. *Person to person.* 3rd ed. Baltimore: Paul H. Brookes Publishing.

Hutchison, P., and J. McGill. 1998. *Leisure, integration and community.* 2nd ed. Toronto: Leisurability Publications.

Kraus, R., and J. Shank. 1992. *Therapeutic recreation service: Principles and practices.* 4th ed. Dubuque, IA: Brown.

Leitner, M.J., and S.F. Leitner. 2004. *Leisure in later life.* 3rd ed. New York: Haworth.

McGill, J. 1996. *Leisure identities.* Toronto: Leisurability Publications.

McGuire, F.A., R. Boyd, and R.E. Tedrick. 2004. *Leisure and aging.* 3rd ed. Champaign, IL: Sagamore Publishing.

National Therapeutic Recreation Society (NTRS). 1993. *The best of the Therapeutic Recreation Journal: Aging.* Arlington, VA: National Recreation and Park Association.

O'Morrow, G.S., and M.J. Carter. 1997. *Effective management in the therapeutic recreation service.* State College, PA: Venture Publishing.

Paciorek, M.J., and J.A. Jones. 1989. *Sports and recreation for the disabled.* Indianapolis: Benchmark Press.

Peterson, C.P., and N.J. Stumbo. 2004. *Therapeutic recreation program design: Principles and procedures.* 4th ed. Boston: Allyn & Bacon.

Rainwater, A.B. 1992. *Therapeutic recreation for chemically dependent adolescents and adults: Programming and activities.* Reston, VA: American Alliance for Health, Physical Education, Recreation and Dance.

Riley, B., ed. 1991. *Quality management: Applications for therapeutic recreation.* State College, PA: Venture Publishing.

Schleien, S.J., M. Tipton Ray, and F. Green. 1997. *Community recreation and persons with disabilities: Strategies for integration.* Baltimore: Paul H. Brookes Publishing.

Shephard, R.J. 1997. *Aging, physical activity, and health.* Champaign, IL: Human Kinetics.

Sherrill, C. 1998. *Adapted physical activity, recreation and sport: Cross disciplinary and lifespan.* 5th ed. Dubuque, IA: Brown & Benchmark.

Smith, R.W., D.R. Austin, and D.W. Kennedy. 2001. *Inclusive and special recreation, opportunities for persons with disabilities.* 4th ed. Dubuque, IA: Brown & Benchmark.

Spirduso, W.W. 1995. *Physical dimensions of aging.* Champaign, IL: Human Kinetics.

Stensrud, C. 1993. *A training manual for Americans with Disabilities Act compliance in parks and recreation settings.* State College, PA: Venture Publishing.

Stewart, D.A. 1991. *Deaf sport.* Washington, DC: Gallaudet University Press.

Stumbo, N.J., ed. 2003. *Client outcomes in therapeutic recreation services.* State College, PA: Venture Publishing.

Stumbo, N.J., and C.A. Peterson. 2004. *Therapeutic recreation program design.* 4th ed. San Francisco: Pearson Education (Benjamin Cummings).

Sylvester, C., J.E. Voelkl, and G.D. Ellis. 2001. *Therapeutic recreation programming: Theory and practice.* State College, PA: Venture Publishing.

Teague, M.L., and R.D. MacNeil. 1992. *Aging and leisure.* 2nd ed. Dubuque, IA: Brown & Benchmark.

Winslow, R.M., and K.J. Halberg, eds. 1992. *The management of therapeutic recreation services.* Arlington, VA: National Recreation and Park Association.

Witt, P., and J. Crompton, eds. 1996. *Recreation programs that work for at-risk youth.* State College, PA: Venture Publishing.

An abridged edition is available from National Recreation and Park Association (NRPA).

YMCA of the USA. 1991. *Programs for special populations.* YMCA Program Discovery Series, vol. 2, no. 3., Champaign, IL: Human Kinetics.

SPORT MANAGEMENT, PHYSICAL ACTIVITY, AND FITNESS

This list includes resources on sport management from a leisure and recreation perspective. It does not include resources on sport and fitness activities or on the conduct of scientific research about exercise and physical activity. See also the section on Therapeutic Recreation on page 119, the section on Management and Administration on page 129, and the section on Areas, Facilities, and Urban Park Planning on page 131.

Appenzeller, H., and G. Lewis, eds. 2000. *Successful sport management.* 2nd ed. Durham, NC: Carolina Academic Press.

Bar-Or, O. 1996. *The child and adolescent athlete.* Cambridge, MA: Blackwell Science.

Begel, D., and R.W. Burton, eds. 2000. *Sport psychiatry.* New York: Norton

Birell, S., and C.L. Cole. 1994. *Women, sport and culture.* Champaign, IL: Human Kinetics.

Bouchard, C., R.J. Shephard, and T. Stephens. 1994. *Physical activity, fitness, and health.* Champaign, IL: Human Kinetics.
International Proceedings and Consensus Statement.

Brooks, C.M. 1994. *Sports marketing, competitive business strategies for sports.* Englewood Cliffs, NJ: Prentice Hall.

Brown, S.C., and L. Schoonmaker, eds. 1999. *Managing the collegiate recreational facility.* Corvallis, OR: National Intramural-Recreational Sports Association.

Carpenter, L.J. 2000. *Legal concepts in sport.* 2nd ed. Champaign, IL: Sagamore Publishing.

Carron, A.V., and H.A. Hausenblas. 1998. *Group dynamics in sport.* 2nd ed. Morgantown, WV: Fitness Information Technology.

Cohen, G.L., ed. 2001. *Women in sport: Issues and controversies.* Reston, VA: National Association for Girls and Women in Sports.

Collingwood, T.R. 1997. *Helping at-risk youth through physical fitness programming.* Champaign, IL: Human Kinetics.

Cotten, D., and J.T. Wolohan, eds. 2003. *Law for recreation and sport managers.* 3rd ed. Dubuque, IA: Kendall/Hunt.

Csikszentmihalyi, M. 1999. *Flow in sports.* Champaign, IL: Human Kinetics.

Curtis, J.E., and S.J. Russell, eds. 1997. *Physical activity in human experience: Interdisciplinary perspectives.* Champaign, IL: Human Kinetics.

DeSensi, J.T., and D. Rosenberg. 1996. *Ethics in sport management.* Sport Management Library series. Morgantown, WV: Fitness Information Technology.

Dishman, R.K., ed. 1994. *Advances in exercise adherence.* Champaign, IL: Human Kinetics.

Doughtery, N.J., A. Goldberger, and L.J. Carpenter. 2002. *Sport, physical activity, and the law.* 2nd ed. Champaign, IL: Sagamore Publishing.

Farmer, P.J., A.L. Mulrooney, and R. Annon. 1996. *Sport facility planning and management.* Morgantown, WV: Fitness Information Technology (Sport Management Library).

Grantham, W.C., et al. 1998. *Health fitness management.* Champaign, IL: Human Kinetics.

Horne, J., A. Tomlinson, and G. Whannel. 1999. *Understanding sport: An introduction to the sociological and cultural analysis of sport.* New York: Routledge.

Howard, D.R., and J.L. Crompton. 1995. *Financing sport.* Morgantown, WV: Fitness Information Technology (Sport Management Library).

Langley, T.D., and J.D. Hawkins. 2004. *Administration for exercise-related professions.* 2nd ed. Belmont, CA: Thomson Learning/Wadsworth.

Lapchick, R.E. 1996. *Sport in society: Equal opportunity or business as usual?* Thousand Oaks, CA: Sage Publications.

Leith, L.M. 1994. *Foundations of exercise and mental health.* Morgantown, WV: Fitness Information Technology.

Masteralexis, L.P., C.A. Barr, and M.A. Hums. 1998. *Principles and practice of sport management.* Gaithersburg, MD: Aspen.

McMurray, R.G. 1999. *Concepts in fitness programming.* Boca Raton, FL: CRC Press.

Miller, L.K. 1997. *Sport business management.* Gaithersburg, MD: Aspen.

Mull, R.F., et al. 1997. *Recreational sport management,* 3rd ed. Champaign, IL: Human Kinetics.

Mullin, B.J., S. Hardy, and W.A. Sutton. 2000. *Sport marketing.* 2nd ed. Champaign, IL: Human Kinetics.

Olson, J.R. 1997. *Facility and equipment management for sport directors.* Champaign, IL: Human Kinetics.

Parkhouse, B.L., ed. 2004. *The management of sport: Its foundation and application.* 4th ed. St. Louis: Mosby.

Parks, J.B., B. Zanger, and J. Quarterman, eds. 1998. *Contemporary sport management.* Champaign, IL: Human Kinetics.

Pitts, B.G., and D.K. Stotlar. 1996. *Fundamentals of sport marketing.* Morgantown, WV: Fitness Information Technology.

Roberts, G.C., ed. 1992. *Motivation in sport and exercise.* Champaign, IL: Human Kinetics.

Sawyer, T., and O. Smith. 1999. *The management of clubs, recreation, and sport: Concepts and applications.* Champaign, IL: Sagamore Publishing.

Seefeldt, V., and E.W. Brown, eds. 1991. *Program for athletic coaches' education (PACE).* Carmel, IN: Benchmark Press
For youth sport coaches.

Serpa, S., J. Alves, and V. Pataco. 1994. *International perspectives on sport and exercise psychology.* Morgantown, WV: Fitness Information Technology.

Singer, R.N., H.A. Hausenblas, and C.M. Janelle, eds. 2001. *Handbook of sport psychology.* 2nd ed. New York: Wiley.

Slack, T. 1997. *Understanding sport organizations.* Champaign, IL: Human Kinetics.

Smoll, F.L., and R.E. Smith. 1996. *Children and youth in sport: A biopsychosocial perspective.* Dubuque, IA: Brown & Benchmark.

Stier, W.F. 1999. *Managing sport, fitness, and recreation programs.* Boston: Allyn & Bacon.

Tharrett, S.J., and J.A. Peterson. 1997. *ACSM's health/fitness facility standards and guidelines.* 2nd ed. Champaign, IL: Human Kinetics.

Tillman, K.G., E.F. Voltmer, A.A. Esslinger, and B. McCue. 1996. *The administration of physical education, sport and leisure programs.* Needham Heights, MA: Allyn & Bacon.

Walker, M.L., and D.K. Stotlar. 1997. *Sport facility management.* Boston: Jones & Bartlett Publishers.

Weinberg, R.S., and D. Gould. 1995. *Foundations of sport and exercise psychology.* Champaign, IL: Human Kinetics.

COMMERCIAL RECREATION AND TOURISM

This section includes resources on employee recreation.

Abram, S., J. Waldren, and D.V.L. Macleod. 1997. *Tourists and tourism: Identifying with people and places.* Ethnicity and Identity Series. New York: Berg.

Ashworth, G.J., and J.E. Tunbridge. 2000. *The tourist-historic city: Retrospect and prospect of managing the heritage city.* Advances in Tourism Research Series. New York: Pergamon Press.

Borocz, J., ed. 1996. *Leisure migration: A sociological study on tourism.* Tourism Social Science Series. New York: Elsevier Science (Pergamon Press).

Bosselman, F.P., C.A. Peterson, and C. McCarthy. 1999. *Managing tourism growth: Issues and applications.* Washington, DC: Island Press.

Bramwell, B., and B. Lane, eds. 2000. *Tourism collaboration and partnership.* Aspects of Tourism, No. 2. Tonawanda, NY: Channel View Publications.

Burns, P.M. 1999. *An introduction to tourism and anthropology.* New York: Routledge.

Busser, J.A. 1990. *Programming for employee services and recreation.* Champaign, IL: Sagamore Publishing.

Butler, R., C.M. Hall, and J. Jenkins, eds. 1998. *Tourism and recreation in rural areas.* New York: Wiley.

Cabot, A.N. 1996. *Casino gaming: Policy, economics, and regulation.* Las Vegas, NV: UNLV International Gaming Institute.

Chambers, E., ed. 1997. *Tourism and culture.* Albany, NY: State University of New York Press.

Chon, K.S., T. Inagaki, and T. Ohashi, eds. 2000. *Japanese tourist: Socio-economic, marketing and psychological analysis.* New York: Haworth.

Crossley, J.C., L.M. Jamieson, and R.E. Brayley. 2001. *Introduction to commercial recreation and tourism: An entrepreneurial approach.* 4th ed. Champaign, IL: Sagamore Publishing.

Crotts, J.C., and W.F. van Raaij, eds. 1994. *Economic psychology of travel and tourism.* New York: Haworth.

Eagles, P.F.J., and S.F. McCool. 2002. *Tourism in national parks and protected areas: Planning and management.* New York: CABI Publishing.

Edgell, D.L. 1999. *Tourism policy: The next millennium.* Advances in Tourism Applications, vol. 3. Champaign, IL: Sagamore Publishing.

Fennell, D.A. 1999. *Ecotourism: An introduction.* New York: Routledge.

Font, X., and J. Tribe, eds. 2000. *Forest tourism and recreation.* New York: CABI Publishing.

Fridgen, J.D. 1996. *Tourism and the hospitality industry.* East Lansing, MI: Educational Institute of the American Hotel and Lodging Association.

   Initially issued in 1991 as Dimensions of Tourism.

Gartner, W.C. 1996. *Tourism development, principles, processes, and policies.* New York: Van Nostrand Reinhold.

Getz, D. 1997. *Event management and event tourism.* New York: Cognizant Communication.

Godfrey, K., and J. Clarke. 2000. *The tourism development handbook.* New York: Continuum.

Goeldner, C.R., J.R.B. Ritchie, and R.W. McIntosh. 2000. *Tourism principles, practices, philosophies.* 8th ed. New York: Wiley.

Hall, C.M., and S.J. Page. 1999. *The geography of tourism and recreation: Environment, place and space.* New York: Routledge.

Huan, T.C., and J.T. O'Leary. 1999. *Measuring tourism performance.* Advances in Tourism Applictions Series, vol. 1. Champaign, IL: Sagamore Publishing.

Hawkins, D.E., J.R.B. Ritchie, F. Go, and D. Frechtling, eds. 1992. *World travel and tourism review: Indicators, trends and forecasts,* vols. 1 and 2. Wallingford, Oxon, UK: CABI Publishing.

Heidrich, K.W. 1991. *Working with volunteers in employee services and recreation programs.* Champaign, IL: Sagamore Publishing.

Hoff, M.K., ed. 2001. *Community tourism development.* St. Paul: University of Minnesota Extension Service.

Honey, M. 1999. *Ecotourism and sustainable development.* Washington, DC: Island Press

Hudson, S., ed. 2003. *Sport and adventure tourism.* New York: Haworth.

Lanfant, M.F., J.B. Allcock, and E.M. Bruner, eds. 1995. *International tourism: Identity and change.* Thousand Oaks, CA: Sage Publications.

Lindberg, K., and D. Hawkins, eds. 1993. *Ecotourism: A guide for planners and managers.* (Volume 1). North Bennington, VT: Ecotourism Society.

Lindberg, K., M. Wood, and D. Engeldrum, eds. 1998. *Ecotourism: A guide for planners and managers.* (Volume 2). North Bennington, VT: Ecotourism Society.

McCool, S., and A.E. Watson, comps. 1995. Linking tourism, the environment, and sustainability. (Compiled papers, 1994, National Recreation and Parks Association [NRPA].) Forest Service Intermountain Research Station, General Technical Report INT-GTR-3323.

McIntosh, R.W., C.R. Goeldner, and J.R.B. Ritchie. 1995. *Tourism: Principles, practices, philosophies.* 7th ed. New York: Wiley.

McKercher, B., and H. duCros. 2002. *Cultural tourism: The partnership between tourism and cultural heritage management.* Binghampton, NT: Haworth Hospitality Press.

Moscardo, G. 1999. *Making visitors mindful: Principles for creating sustainable visitor experiences through effective communication.* Advances in Tourism Applications Series, vol. 2. Champaign, IL: Sagamore Publishing.

Murphy, P.E., ed. 1997. *Quality management in urban tourism.* New York: Wiley.

Noe, F. 1999. *Tourist service satisfaction: Hotel, transportation, and recreation.* Advances in Tourism Applications Series, vol. 5. Champaign, IL: Sagamore Publishing.

Nykiel, R.A., and E. Jascolt, 1998. *Marketing your city, U.S.A.* New York: Haworth.

Opperman, M., ed. 1997. *Geography and tourism marketing.* New York: Haworth.

Orams, M. 1999. *Marine tourism, development, impacts and management.* New York: Routledge.

Pearce, P.L., G. Moscardo, and G.F. Ross. 1996. *Tourism community relationships.* Tourism Social Science Series. New York: Elsevier Science (Pergamon Press).

Pindroh, R.A. 1996. *Employee services, a strategic component of business.* Champaign, IL: Sagamore Publishing.

Reich, A. 1999. *Positioning of tourist destinations.* Advances in Tourism Applications Series, vol. 4. Champaign, IL: Sagamore Publishing.

Ritchie, J.R.B., and C.R. Goeldner. 1994. *Travel tourism and hospitality research: A handbook for managers and researchers.* New York: Wiley.

Ryan, C. 1991. *Recreational tourism: A social science perspective.* London: Routledge & Kegan Paul.

Sawyer, T.H. 2001. *Employee services management.* Champaign, IL: Sagamore Publishing.

Schwanke, D., et al. 1997. *Resort development handbook.* Washington, DC: Urban Land Institute.

Scott, J.T. 1998. *Fundamentals of leisure business success: A manager's guide to achieving success in the leisure and recreation industry.* New York: Haworth.

Shakley, M. 1996. *Wildlife tourism.* Boston: International Thomson Business Press.

Sinclair, M.T., and M. Stabler. 1997. *The economics of tourism.* London: Routledge & Kegan Paul.

Smith, V.L., and W.R. Eadington, eds. 1992. *Tourism alternatives: Potentials and problems in the development of tourism.* Philadelphia: University of Pennsylvania Press.

Song, H., and S.F. Witt. 2000. *Tourism demand modeling and forecasting: Modern ecometric approaches.* Advances in Tourism Research Series. New York: Pergamon Press.

Standeven, J., and P. De Knop. 1999. *Sport tourism.* Champaign, IL: Human Kinetics.

Thompson, J.L., et al., comps. 1995. *Fourth International Outdoor Recreation and Tourism Trends Symposium.* St. Paul: University of Minnesota.

Towner, J. 1996. *An historical geography of recreation and tourism in the Western world 1540-1940.* New York: Wiley.

U.S. Travel and Tourism Administration (USTTA). 1993. *World tourism at the millennium: An agenda for industry, government, and education.* Washington, DC: U.S. Department of Commerce.

Urry, J. 1990. *The tourist gaze: Leisure and travel in contemporary societies.* Newbury Park, CA: Sage Publications.

Veal, A.J., P. Johnson, and G. Cushman. 1993. *Leisure and Tourism: Social and Environmental Change.* (Papers 1991 WLRA Congress.) Sharbot Lake, ON: World Leisure and Recreation Association.

Vukonic, B. 1996. *Tourism and religion.* Tourism Social Science Series. New York: Elsevier Science (Pergamon Press).

Wang, N. 2000. *Tourism and modernity: A sociological analysis.* Tourism Social Science Series. New York: Elsevier Science (Pergamon Press).

Weber, K., and K.S. Chon, eds. 2002. *Convention tourism: International research and industry perspectives.* New York: Haworth.

Weston, S.A. 1995. *Commercial recreation & tourism: An introduction to business orientation recreation (commercial recreation).* Dubuque, IA: McGraw-Hill Higher Education.

Whelan, T., ed. 1991. *Nature tourism: Managing for the environment.* Washington, DC: Island Press.

Whitlock, W., K. Van Romer, and R.H. Becker. 1991. *Nature based tourism: An annotated bibliography.* Strom Thurmond Institute of Government and Public Affairs, Clemson University.

Williams, A.M., and G. Shaw, eds. 1991. *Tourism and economic development: Western european experiences.* 2nd ed. New York: Belhaven Press.

Witt, S.F., and L. Moutinho, eds. 1994. *Tourism marketing and management handbook.* 2nd ed. New York: Prentice-Hall.

Woodside, A.G., et al., eds. 2000. *Consumer psychology of tourism, hospitality, and leisure.* New York: CABI Publishing.

Wyllie, R.W. 2000. *Tourism and society: A guide to problems and issues.* State College, PA: Venture Publishing.

Yu, L. 1999. *The international hospitality business, management, and operations.* New York: Haworth.

Zerger, J.B., and L.M. Caneday, eds. 1991. *Tourism and leisure: Dynamics and diversity.* Alexandria, VA: National Recreation and Park Association.

EVALUATION AND RESEARCH METHODOLOGY AND STATISTICS

This section includes resources on action research, focus groups, and needs assessment.

Adler, E., and R. Clark. 2003. *How it's done: An invitation to social research.* Belmont, CA: Wadsworth/Thomson Learning.

Agere, S., and N. Jorm. 2000. *Designing performance appraisals: Assessing needs and designing performance management systems in the public sector.* London: Commonwealth Secretariat.

Alreck, P.L. 1995. *The survey research handbook.* 2nd ed. Chicago: Irwin Professional Publishing.

Altschuld, J.W., and B.R. Witkin. 2000. *From needs assessment to action.* Thousand Oaks, CA: Sage Publications.

Babbie, E. 1998. *The practice of social research.* 8th ed. Belmont, CA: Wadsworth.

Barnett, L.A. 1995. *Research about leisure: Past, present, and future.* 2nd ed. Champaign, IL: Sagamore Publishing.

Bartholomew, D.J. 1996. *The statistical approach to social measurement.* San Diego: Academic Press.

Baumgartner, T.A., C.H. Strong, and L.D. Hensley. 2002. *Conducting and reading research in health and human performance.* 3rd ed. New York: McGraw-Hill.

Bearden, W.O., R.G. Netemeyer, and M.F. Mobley. 1999. *Handbook of marketing scales: Multi-item measures for marketing and consumer behavior research.* 2nd ed. Newbury Park, CA: Sage Publications.

Berg, K.E., and R.W. Latin. 2004. *Essentials of research methods in health, physical education, exercise science, and recreation.* 2nd ed. Philadelphia: Lippincott, Williams & Wilkins.

Bickman, L., and D.J. Rog, eds. 1998. *Handbook of applied social research methods.* Thousand Oaks, CA: Sage Publications.

Biemer, P.P. and others, eds. 1991. *Measurement errors in surveys.* New York: Wiley.

Blaike, N. 2003. *Analyzing quantitative data from description to explanation.* Thousand Oaks, CA: Sage Publications.

Blalock, A.B., ed. 1990. *Evaluating social programs at the state and local level.* Kalamazoo, MI: W.E. Upjohn Institute for Employment Research.

Bogdan, R.C., and S. Knopp Biklen. 2003. *Qualitative research for education: An introduction to theory and methods.* 4th ed. Boston: Allyn & Bacon.

Browne, M.N., and S. Kelley. 2001. *Asking the right questions: A guide to critical thinking.* 6th ed. Upper Saddle River, NJ: Prentice-Hall.

Burdge, R.J. 1998. *A conceptual approach to social impact assessment.* Rev. ed. Middleton, WI: Social Ecology Press.

Burdge, R.J. 1999. *A community guide to social impact assessment.* Rev. ed. Middleton, WI: Social Ecology Press.

Burlingame, J., and T.M. Blascho. 2002. *Assessment tools for recreational therapy and related fields.* 3rd ed. Ravensdale, WA: Idyll Arbor.

Chambliss, D.F., and R.K. Schutt. 2003. *Making sense of the social world: Methods of investigation.* Thousand Oaks, CA: Sage Publications.

Chirban, J.T. 1996. *Interviewing in depth.* Thousand Oaks, CA: Sage Publications.

Church, A., and J. Waclawski. 1998. *Designing and using organizational surveys.* San Francisco: Jossey-Bass.

Churchill, G.A., Jr. 1999. *Marketing research: Methodological foundations.* 7th ed. Chicago: Dryden Press.

Coffey, A., and P. Atkinson. 1996. *Making sense of qualitative data: Complementary research strategies.* Thousand Oaks, CA: Sage Publications.

Coghlan, D., and T. Brannick. 2001. *Doing action research in your own organization.* Thousand Oaks, CA: Sage Publications.

Crabtree, B.F., and W.L. Miller, eds. 1999. *Doing qualitative research.* 2nd ed. Thousand Oaks, CA: Sage Publications.

Creswell, J.W. 1998. *Qualitative inquiry and research design: Choosing among five traditions.* Thousand Oaks, CA: Sage Publications.

Creswell, J.W. 2002. *Research design: Qualitative and quantitative approaches.* 2nd ed. Thousand Oaks, CA: Sage Publications.

Cunningham, J.B. 1993. *Action research and organizational development.* Westport, CT: Praeger.

Czarnecki, M.T. 1999. *Managing by measuring: How to improve your organization's performance through effective benchmarking.* New York: American Management Association.

Denzin, N.K., and Y.S. Lincoln, eds. 2005. *Handbook of qualitative research.* 3rd ed. Thousand Oaks, CA: Sage Publications.

Dillman, D.A. 2000. *Mail and Internet surveys: The tailored design method.* 2nd ed. New York: Wiley.

Donaldson, S., and M. Scriven, eds. 2003. *Evaluating social programs and problems.* Mahway, NJ: Lawrence Associates.

Dunaway, D.K., and W.K. Baum, eds. 1996. *Oral history: An interdisciplinary anthology.* 2nd ed. Walnut Creek, CA: AltaMira Press.

  Published in cooperation with the American Association for State and Local History and the Oral History Association.

Easterby-Smith, M., R. Thorpe, and A. Lowe. 1991. *Management research: An introduction.* Newbury Park, CA: Sage Publications.

Fern, E.F. 2001. *Advanced focus group research.* Thousand Oaks, CA: Sage Publications.

Fink, A., ed. 2002. *The survey kit.* 2nd ed. Thousand Oaks, CA: Sage Publications.

  The series is composed of nine small volumes.

Folz, D.H. 1996. *Survey research for public administration.* Thousand Oaks, CA: Sage Publications.

Gall, M.D., J.P. Gall, and W.R. Borg. 2003. *Educational research.* 7th ed. Boston: Allyn & Bacon.

Gray, S.T. and associates. 1998. *Evaluation with power: A new approach to organizational effectiveness, empowerment, and excellence.* San Francisco: Jossey-Bass.

Greenbaum, T.L. 2000. *Moderating focus groups.* Thousand Oaks, CA: Sage Publications.

Gubrium, J.F., and A. Sankar, eds. 1994. *Qualitative methods in aging research.* Thousand Oaks, CA: Sage Publications.

Gummesson, E. 2000. *Qualitative methods in management research.* 2nd ed. Thound Oaks, CA: Sage Publications.

Hale, R., and P. Whitlam. 2000. *Powering up performance management.* Burlington, VT: Gower.

Harrington, H.J., and J.S. Harrington. 1996. *High performance benchmarking.* New York: McGraw-Hill.

Henderson, K.A. 1991. *Dimensions of choice: A qualitative approach to recreation, parks, and leisure research.* State College, PA: Venture Publishing.

Henderson, K.A. 2002. *Evaluating leisure services: Making enlightened decisions.* 2nd ed. State College, PA: Venture Publishing.

Henry, G.T. 1995. *Graphing data: Techniques for display and analysis.* Applied Social Research Methods Series, vol. 36. Thousand Oaks, CA: Sage Publications.

Holloway, J., J. Lewis, and G. Mallor. 1995. *Performance measurement and evaluation.* Thousand Oaks, CA: Sage Publications (with The Open University).

Huck, S.W. 2004. *Reading statistics and research.* 4th ed. Boston: Pearson Education.

Jason, L.A., et al., eds. *Participatory community research.* 2004. Washington, DC: American Psychological Association.

Jones, S. 1999. *Doing Internet research.* Thousand Oaks, CA: Sage Publications.

Kaydos, W. 1999. *Operational performance measurement.* Baton Rouge, FL: CRC Press.

Kelly, J.R., and R.B. Warnick. 1999. *Recreation trends and markets.* Champaign, IL: Sagamore Publishing.

Kraus, R., and L. Allen. 1997. *Research and evaluation in recreation, parks, and leisure studies.* 2nd ed. Columbus, OH: Publishing Horizons.

Kraut, A.I., ed. 1996. *Organizational surveys: Tools for assessment and change.* San Francisco: Jossey-Bass.

Krueger, R.A., and M.A. Casey. 2000. *Focus groups: A practical guide for applied research.* 3rd ed. Thousand Oaks, CA: Sage Publications.

Kvale, S. 1996. *InterViews: An introduction to qualitative research interviewing.* Thousand Oaks, CA: Sage Publications.

Malkin, M.J., and C.Z. Howe, eds. 1993. *Research in therapeutic recreation: Concepts and methods.* State College, PA: Venture Publishing.

Mangione, T.W. 1995. *Mail surveys: Improving the quality.* Applied Social Research Methods Series, vol. 40. Thousand Oaks, CA: Sage Publications.

Mark, M.M., G.T. Henry, and G. Julnes. 2000. *Evaluation: An integrated framework for understanding, guiding and improving public and nonprofit policies and programs.* San Francisco: Jossey-Bass.

Marshall, C., and G.B. Rossman. 1995. *Designing qualitative research.* 2nd ed. Thousand Oaks, CA: Sage Publications.

Martin, L.L., and P.M. Kettner. 1996. *Measuring the performance of human service programs.* Sage Human Services Guides, vol. 71. Thousand Oaks, CA: Sage Publications.

Maxwell, J.A. 1996. *Qualitative research design: An interactive approach.* Applied Social Research Methods Series, vol. 41. Thousand Oaks, CA: Sage Publications.

Merriam, S.B. and associates. 2002. *Qualitative research in practice: Examples for discussion and analysis.* San Francisco: Jossey-Bass.

Miles, M.B., and A.M. Huberman. 1994. *Qualitative data analysis: An expanded sourcebook.* 2nd ed. Thousand Oaks, CA: Sage Publications.

Miller, D.C., and N.J. Salkind. 2002. *Handbook of research design and social measurement.* 6th ed. Newbury Park, CA: Sage Publications.

Miller, G., and R. Dingwall, eds. 1997. *Context and method in qualitative research.* Thousand Oaks, CA: Sage Publications.

Miller, G.J., and M.L. Whicker. 1999. *Handbook of research methods in public administration.* New York: Marcel Dekker.

Miller, T.I., and M.A. Miller. 1991. *Citizen surveys: How to do them, how to use them, what they mean.* Washington, D.C.: International City/County Management Association.

Mitra, A., and S. Lankford. 1999. *Research methods in park, recreation, and leisure services.* Champaign, IL: Sagamore Publishing.

Mohr, L.B. 1992. *Impact analysis for program evaluation.* Newbury Park, CA: Sage Publications.

Morgan, D.L. 1997. *Focus groups as qualitative research.* 2nd ed. Qualitative Research Methods Series, vol. 16. Thousand Oaks, CA: Sage Publications.

Morgan, D.L., and R.A. Krueger. 1998. *The focus group kit.* Thousand Oaks, CA: Sage Publications. *The kit contains six small volumes.*

Morrow, J.R., et al. 2000. *Measurement and evaluation in human performance.* 2nd ed. Champaign, IL: Human Kinetics.

National Therapeutic Recreation Society (NTRS). 1996. *The best of the Therapeutic Recreation Journal: Assessments.* Ashburn, VA: National Recreation and Park Association.

Nicol, A.M., and P.M. Pexman. 2003. *Displaying your findings: A practical guide for creating figures, posters, and presentations.* Washington, DC: American Psychological Association.

Nicol, A.M., and P.M. Pexman. 2003 (updates). *Presenting your findings: A practical guide for creating tables.* Washington, DC: American Psychological Association.

Niven, P.R. 2002. *Balanced scorecard: Step-by-step.* New York: Wiley.

Noffke, S.E., and R.B. Stevenson, eds. 1995. *Educational action research: Becoming practically critical.* New York: Teachers College Press, Columbia University Press.

Organizations for Economic Cooperation and Development. 1996. *Performance auditing and the modernization of government.* Paris: OECD.

Patton, C.V., and D.S. Sawicki. 1986. *Basic methods of policy analysis and planning.* Upper Saddle River, NJ: Prentice-Hall.

Patton, M.Q. 2002. *Qualitative research and evaluation methods.* Thousand Oaks, CA: Sage Publications.

Popham, W.J., and K.A. Sirotnik. 1992. *Understanding statistics in education.* Itasca, IL: Peacock.

Posavac, E.J., and R.G. Carey. 1997. *Program evaluation, methods and case studies.* 5th ed. Upper Saddle River, NJ: Prentice-Hall.

Rea, L.M., and R.A. Parker. 1997. *Designing and conducting survey research: A comprehensive guide.* 2nd ed. San Francisco: Jossey-Bass.

Reason, P., and H. Bradbury, eds. 2001. *Handbook of action research: Participative inquiry and practice.* Thousand Oaks, CA: Sage Publications.

Riddick, C., and R. Russell. 1999. *Evaluative research in recreation, park, and sport settings: Searching for useful information.* Champaign, IL: Sagamore Publishing.

Ritchie, J.R.B., and C.R. Goeldner. 1994. *Travel, tourism, and hospitality research.* 2nd ed. New York: Wiley.

Robinson, J.P., P.R. Shaver, and L.S. Wrightsman, eds. 1991. *Measures of personality and social psychological attitudes.* San Diego: Academic Press.

Rosenthal, R., and R. Rosnow. 1991. *Essentials of behavioral research: Methods and data analysis.* 2nd ed. New York: McGraw-Hill.

Rossi, H.P., H.E. Freeman, and M.W. Lipsay. 2004. *Evaluation: A systematic approach.* 7th ed. Newbury Park, CA: Sage Publications.

Rubin, A., and E. Babbie. 2004. *Research methods for social work.* 5th ed. Belmont, CA: Wadsworth/Thomson Learning.

Rubin, H.J., and I.S. Rubin. 1995. *Qualitative interviewing: The art of hearing data.* Thousand Oaks, CA: Sage Publications.

Russ-Eft, D., and H. Preskill. 2001. *Evaluation in organizations.* Cambridge, MA: Perseus Publishing.

Schalock, R.L. 1995. *Outcome-based evaluation.* New York: Plenum Press.

Schuman, H., and S. Presser. 1996. *Questions and answers in attitude surveys.* Thousand Oaks, CA: Sage Publications.

Schut, R.K. 2001. *Investigating the social world: The process and practice of research.* 3rd ed. Thousand Oaks, CA: Sage Publications.

Seale, C. 1999. *The quality of qualitative research.* Thousand Oaks, CA: Sage Publications.

Shadish, W.R., Jr., T.D. Coo, and L.C. Leviton. 1991. *Foundations of program evaluation: Theories of practice.* Newbury Park, CA: Sage Publications.

Shaw, I. 1999. *Qualitative research.* Thousand Oaks, CA: Sage Publications.

Sheskin, D.J. 2000. *Handbook of parametric and nonparametric statistical procedures.* 2nd ed. Boca Raton, FL: CRC Press.

Shockley, J.M., Jr. 1995. *Research and data analysis in leisure, recreation, tourism and sport management.* Las Vegas, NV: Sigma Press.

Sirkin, R.M. 1995. *Statistics for the social sciences.* Thousand Oaks, CA: Sage Publications.

Stringer, E.T. 1999. *Action research: A handbook for practitioners.* 2nd ed. Thousand Oaks, CA: Sage Publications.

Templeton, J.F. 1994. *The focus group.* Rev. ed. Burr Ridge, IL: Irwin Publishing.

Thomas, J.R., and J.K. Nelson. 2001. *Research methods in physical activity.* 4th ed. Champaign, IL: Human Kinetics.

Thompson, N.J., and H.O. McClintock. 1998. *Demonstrating your program's worth.* Atlanta: National Center for Injury Prevention and Control.

United Way of America. 1996. *Measuring program outcomes: A practical approach.* Alexandria, VA: United Way of America.

Vaughn, S., J.S. Schumm, and J. Sinagub. 1996. *Focus group interviews in education and psychology.* Thousand Oaks, CA: Sage Publications.

Wallgren, A., et al. 1996. *Graphing statistics and data: Creating better charts.* Thousand Oaks, CA: Sage Publications.

Weisberg, H., and B. Brown. 1996. *An introduction to survey research polling and data analysis.* 3rd ed. Thousand Oaks, CA: Sage Publications.

Weiss, C.H. 1998. *Evaluation: Methods for studying programs and policies.* 2nd ed. Upper Saddle River, NJ: Prentice-Hall.

Wholey, J.S., H.P. Hatry, and K.E. Newcomer, eds. 1994. *Handbook of practical program evaluation.* San Francisco: Jossey-Bass.

Witkin, B.R., and J.W. Altschuld. 1995. *Planning and conducting needs assessment.* Thousand Oaks, CA: Sage Publications.

Wolcott, H.F. 2001. *Writing up qualitative research.* Thousand Oaks, CA: Sage Publications.

Worthen, B.R., J.R. Saunders, and J.L. Fitzpatrick. 1997. *Program evaluation: Alternative approaches and practical guidelines.* 2nd ed. White Plains, NY: Longman Publications.

Yin, R.K. 1994. *Case study research: Design and methods.* 2nd ed. Newbury Park, CA: Sage Publications.

Yow, V.R. 1994. *Recording oral history: A practical guide for social scientists.* Thousand Oaks, CA: Sage Publications.

Zalatan, A. 1994. *Forecasting methods in sports and recreation.* Toronto: Thompson Educational Publishing.

Zelazny, G. 1996. *Say it with charts: The executive's guide to visual communication.* 3rd ed. Chicago: Irwin Professional Publishing.

MANAGEMENT AND ADMINISTRATION

For more resources, see also the sections on Sport Management, Physical Activity, and Fitness on page 120 and Natural Resource–Based Recreation Management and Policy on page 133, and the resources at the end of each chapter in *Management of Park and Recreation Agencies* edited by Betty van der Smissen and others.

Allison, M.T., and I.E. Schneider, eds. 2000. *Diversity and the recreation profession: Organizational perspectives.* State College, PA: Venture Publishing.

Alvesson, M. 2002. *Understanding organizational culture.* Thousand Oaks, CA: Sage Publications.

Ashkanasy, N.M., C. Wilderom, and M.F. Peterson, eds. 2000. *Handbook of organizational culture and climate.* Thousand Oaks, CA: Sage Publications.

Bacal, Robert. 1999. *Performance management.* New York: McGraw-Hill.

Bannon, J.J. 1999. *911 management.* Champaign, IL: Sagamore Publishing.

Bannon, J.J., J.A. Busser, and M. Arnold. 2004. *Problem solving in recreation and parks.* 4th ed. Champaign, IL: Sagamore Publishing.

Berman, E.M., et al. 2001. *Human resource management in public service: Paradoxes, processes, and problems.* Thousand Oaks, CA: Sage Publications.

Bingham, R.D., et al. 1991. *Managing local government: Public administration in practice.* Newbury Park, CA: Sage Publications.

Brayley, R.E., and D.D. McLean. 1999. *Managing financial resources in sport and leisure services.* Champaign, IL: Sagamore Publishing.

Brody, R. 2005. *Effectively managing human service organizations.* 3rd ed. Newbury Park, CA: Sage Publications.

Bryson, J.M. 1995. *Strategic planning for public and nonprofit organizations.* Rev. ed. San Francisco: Jossey-Bass.

California Park and Recreation Society (CPRS), comp. 1993. *Tools of the trade.* Sacramento, CA: California Park and Recreation Society.

   This includes a 10-year review of literature in recreation and park management, including searches of Parks & Recreation, Journal of Park and Recreation Administration, and CPRS' Parks and Recreation magazine. It contains more than 40 articles and an 11-page resource directory of other books, organizations, and articles.

Carlson, M., and Alliance for Nonprofit Management (ANM). 2002. *Winning grants: Step by step.* 2nd ed. Nonprofit and Public Management Series. San Francisco: Jossey-Bass.

Chelladurai, P. 1999. *Human resource management in sport and recreation.* Champaign, IL: Human Kinetics.

Cohen, S., and W. Eimicke. 1995. *The new effective public manager: Achieving success in a changing government.* San Francisco: Jossey-Bass.

Commission for Accreditation of Park and Recreation Agencies (CAPRA). 2001. *Self-assessment manual for quality operation of park and recreation agencies.* Ashburn, VA: National Recreation and Park Association.

Connors, T.D., ed. 2001. *The nonprofit handbook: Management.* 3rd ed. New York: Wiley.

Cooper, P.J., and C.A. Newland, eds. 1997. *Handbook of public law and administration.* San Francisco: Jossey-Bass.

Cordes, K.A., and H.M. Ibrahim. 1996. *Applications in recreation and leisure.* St. Louis: Mosby-Year Book.

Crompton, J.L. 1999. *Financing and acquiring park and recreation resources.* Champaign, IL: Human Kinetics.

Daley, D.M. 2002. *Strategic human resource management: People and performance management in the public sector.* New York: Prentice-Hall.

De Waal, A. 2001. *Power of performance management: How leading companies create sustained value.* New York: Wiley.

Dreeszen, C., and P. Korza, eds. 1998. *Fundamentals of local arts management.* Amherst, MA: Arts Extension Service, University of Massachusetts.

Edginton, C.R., S.D. Hudson, and S.V. Lankford. 2001. *Managing recreation, parks, and leisure services: An introduction.* Champaign, IL: Sagamore Publishing.

Fisher, C.D., L.F. Schoenfeldt, and J.B. Shaw. 2003. *Human resource management.* 5th ed. Boston: Houghton Mifflin Company.

Harbour, J.L. 1997. *The basics of performance measurement.* Portland, OR: Productivity Press.

Havitz, M.E., ed., 1995. *Models of change in municipal parks and recreation: A book of innovative case studies.* State College, PA: Venture Publishing.

Herman, R.D. Associates. 1994. *The Jossey-Bass handbook of nonprofit leadership and management.* San Francisco: Jossey-Bass.

Hill, C.W., and G.R. Jones. 2001. *Strategic management: An integrated approach.* 5th ed. Boston: Houghton Mifflin.

Ibrahim, H., and K. Cordes. 2003. *Parks, recreation and leisure service management.* Peosta, IA: Eddie Bowers.

Kaplan, R.S., and D.P. Norton. 2001. *The strategy-focused organization: How balanced scorecard companies thrive in the new business environment.* Boston: Harvard Business School Press.

Kearns, K.P. 2000. *Private sector strategies for social sector success: The guide to strategy and planning for public and nonprofit organizations.* San Francisco: Jossey-Bass.

Kelsey, C., H. Gray, and D. McLean. 2001. *The budget process in parks and recreation: A case study manual.* 3rd ed. Reston, VA: American Association for Leisure and Recreation.

Klein, K. 2001. *Fundraising for social change.* 4th ed. San Francisco: Jossey-Bass

   Part of the Chardon Press series.

Kotler, P., N. Roberto, and N. Lee. 2002. *Social marketing: Improving the quality of life.* 2nd ed. Thousand Oaks, CA: Sage Publications.

Kotler, P. 1982. *Marketing for nonprofit organizations.* 2nd ed. Englewood Cliffs, NJ: Prentice-Hall.

Kraus, R.G., and J.E. Curtis. 2000. *Creative management in recreation, parks, and leisure services.* 6th ed. St. Louis: Mosby.

Linden, R.M. 2002. *Working across boundaries: Making collaboration work in government and nonprofit organizations.* San Francisco: Jossey-Bass.

Loomis, J.B., and R.G. Walsh. 1997. *Recreation economic decisions.* 2nd ed. State College, PA: Venture Publishing.

Malone, T.W. 2004. *The future of work: How the new order of business will shape your organization, your management style, and your life.* Boston: Harvard Business School Press.

Manfredo, M.J., ed. 1992. *Influencing human behavior: Theory and applications in recreation, tourism and natural resources management.* Champaign, IL: Sagamore Publishing.

McCarville, R.E. 2002. *Improving leisure services through marketing action.* Champaign, IL: Sagamore Publishing.

McCurley, S., and R. Lynch. 1996. *Volunteer management.* Downers Grove, IL: Heritage Arts Publishing.

McKinney, W. 1998. *Introduction to park, recreation, and leisure administration.* Champaign, IL: Sagamore Publishing.

McLean, D.D., J.J. Bannon, and H.R. Gray. 1999. *Leisure resources: Its comprehensive planning.* 2nd ed. Champaign, IL: Sagamore Publishing.

Murphy, J.F., et al. 1991. *Leisure systems: Critical concepts and applications.* Champaign, IL: Sagamore Publishing.

Nutt, P.C., and R.W. Backoff. 1991. *Strategic management of public and third sector organizations: A handbook for leaders.* San Francisco: Jossey-Bass.

O'Sullivan, E.L., and M.J. Spangler. 1998. *Experience marketing: Strategies for the new millennium.* State College, PA: Venture Publishing.

O'Sullivan, E.L. 1991. *Marketing for parks, recreation, and leisure.* State College, PA: Venture Publishing.

Perry, J.L., ed. 1996. *Handbook of public administration.* 2nd ed. San Francisco: Jossey-Bass.

Peterson, J.A., and B. Hronek. 2003. *Risk management: Parks, recreation, and leisure services.* 4th ed. Champaign, IL: Sagamore Publishing.

Pfeffer, J., and R. Sutton. 2000. *The knowing–doing gap: How smart companies turn knowledge into action.* Boston: Harvard Business School Press.

Rubin, H. J., and I.S. Rubin. 2001. *Community organizing and development.* 3rd ed. Needham Height, MA: Allyn & Bacon.

Scarborough, N.M., and T.W. Zimmerer. 2002. *Effective small business management.* 7th ed. Englewood Cliffs, NJ: Prentice-Hall.

Schermerhorn, J.R. 2005. *Management.* 8th ed. New York: Wiley.

Shivers, J.S. 1993. *Introduction to recreational service.* Springfield, IL: Charles C. Thomas.

Smith, Bucklin and Assoc. 1994. *The complete guide to nonprofit management.* Eds. R.H. Wilbur, S. Kudla Finn, and C.M. Freeland. New York: Wiley.

Tapping, D., T. Luyster, and T. Shuker. 2002. *Value stream management: Eight steps to planning, mapping, and sustaining lean improvements.* New York: Productivity.

Tedrick, T., and K. Henderson. 1989. *Volunteers in leisure: A management perspective.* Reston, VA: American Alliance for Health, Physical Education, Recreation and Dance.

Turban, E. R. Rainer, and R. Potter. 2004. *Introduction to information technology.* 2nd ed. New York: Wiley.

van der Smissen, B. 1990. *Legal liability and risk management for public and private entities.* Cincinnati: Anderson Publishing.

van der Smissen, B., M. Moiseichik, and V. Hartenburg, eds. 2005. *Management of park and recreation agencies.* 2nd ed. Ashburn, VA: National Recreation and Park Association.
Includes a compendium.

Wade, D., and R. Recardo. 2001. *Corporate performance management: How to build a better organization through measurement-driven strategic alignment.* Boston: Butterworth-Heinemann.

Zairi, M., ed. 1999. *Best practice: Process innovation management.* Boston: Butterworth-Heinemann.

AREAS, FACILITIES, AND URBAN PARK PLANNING

Books on specific facilities such as aquatics and skate parks are not included. See also the section on Sport Management, Physical Activity, and Fitness on page 120.

APPA (Association of Higher Education Facilities Officers). 2001. *Operational guidelines for grounds management.* Alexandria, VA: National Recreation and Park Association, Ashburn, VA; and Professional Grounds Management Society, Baltimore.

ASTM (American Society for Testing and Materials). 1995. *Standard consumer safety performance specifications for playground equipment for public use.* F1487-95. West Conshohocken, PA: ASTM.

ASTM (American Society for Testing and Materials). 2003. *Annual book of ASTM standards.* Section 15, volume 15.07. West Conshohocken, PA: ASTM.

Baud-Bovy, M., and F. Lawson. 1998. *Tourism and recreation handbook of planning and design.* 2nd ed. Boston: Architectural Press.

Christiansen, M.L., ed. 1992. *Play it safe: An anthology on playground safety.* Reston VA: National Recreation and Park Association.

Christiansen, M.L., ed. 1995. *Points about playgrounds.* 2nd ed. Ashburn VA: National Recreation and Park Association.

Dahl, B., and D.J. Molnar. 2003. *Anatomy of a park.* 3rd ed. Prospect Heights, IL: Waveland Press.

Flug, M., and F.A. Klancnik, eds. 1994. *Marinas, parks, and recreation developments.* New York: American Society of Civil Engineers.

Proceedings of the International Conference, Milwaukee, 1994.

Fogg, G., 1990. *Park planning guidelines.* 3rd ed. Arlington, VA: National Recreation and Park Association.

Fogg, G., and FASLA. 2000. *A site design and management process.* Arlington, VA: National Recreation and Park Association.

Fogg, G., and R. Fulton. 1994. *Leisure site guidelines for people over 55.* Arlington, VA: National Recreation and Park Association.

Garvin, A., G. Berens et al. 1997. *Urban parks and open spaces.* Washington, DC: Urban Land Institute.

Gee, C.Y. 1996. *Resort development and management.* 2nd ed. East Lansing, MI: The Educational Institute of the American Hotel and Motel Association.

Glazner, S., coordinator. 2001. *Operational guidelines for grounds management.* Alexandria, VA: APPA (Association of Higher Education Facilities Officers).

Goltsman, S., T. Gilbert, and S. Wohlford. 1993. *The accessibility checklist: An evaluation system for buildings and outdoor settings.* 2nd ed. Berkeley, CA: MIG Communications.

Published in two volumes: User's Guide and Survey Forms.

Harnik, P. 2000. *Inside city parks.* Washington, D.C.: ULI (The Urban Land Institute).

Herbert, D. 1992. *The American Disabilities Act: A guide for health clubs and exercise facilities.* Canton, OH: Professional Reports.

Hultsman, J., R.L. Cottrell, and W.Z. Hultsman. 1998. *Planning parks for people.* 2nd ed. State College, PA: Venture Publishing.

Kutska, K.S., K.J. Hoffman, and A. Malkusk. 2002. *Playground safety is no accident.* 3rd ed. Ashburn, VA: National Recreation and Park Association.

Lagro, J.A. 2001. *Site analysis: Linking program and concept in land planning and design.* New York: Wiley.

McIntyre, S., and S.M. Goltsman. 1997. *Safety first checklist audit and inspection program for children's play areas.* 2nd ed. Berkeley, CA: MIG Communications.

Available from NRPA Publications.

Mertes, J.D., and J.R. Hall. 1996. *Park, recreation, open space and greenway guidelines.* Ashburn, VA: National Recreation and Park Association.

Murrell, D.S., and W.O. Dwyer. 1991. *Constitutional law and liability for park law enforcement officers.* 3rd ed. Durham, NC: Carolina Academic Press.

Sawyer, T.H., ed. 2002. *Facilities planning for health, fitness, physical activity, recreation, and sports: Concepts and application.* 10th ed. Champaign, IL: Sagamore Publishing.

Schwanke, D., et al. 1997. *Resort development handbook.* Washington, DC: Urban Land Institute.

Part of ULI Development Handbook Series.

Schwarz, L., ed. 1993. *Greenways: A guide to planning, design, and development.* Washington, DC: Island Press.

Sharpe, G.W., C.H. Odegaard, and Sharpe, W.F. 1994. *A comprehensive introduction to park management.* 2nd ed. Champaign, IL: Sagamore Publishing.

Sternloff, R.E., and R. Warren. 1993. *Park and recreation maintenance management.* 3rd ed. Scottsdale, AZ: Publishing Horizons.

Tharrett, S.J., and J.A. Peterson, eds. 1997. *Healthy fitness facility standards and guidelines.* 2nd ed. Champaign, IL: Human Kinetics.

U.S. Consumer Product Safety Commission. 1997. *Handbook for public playground safety.* Pub. No. 325. Washington, DC: U.S. Government Printing Office.

Woudstra, J., and K. Fieldhouse, eds. 2000. *The regeneration of public parks.* London and New York: Garden History Society, Landscape Design Trust, and E & FN Spon, with support from English Heritage.

Zelinka, A., and D. Bennan. 2001. *SafeScape: Creating safer, more livable communities through planning and design.* Chicago: Planners Press, American Planning Association.

NATURAL RESOURCE–BASED
RECREATION MANAGEMENT AND POLICY

See also the section on Outdoor and Environment-Related Programs, which starts on page 135.

Aley, J., W. Burch, B. Conover, and D. Field, eds. 1999. *Ecosystem management: Adaptive strategies for natural resources organizations in the twenty-first century.* Philadelphia: Taylor & Francis.

Altman, I., and A. Churchman, eds. 1994. *Women and the environment.* Advances in Theory and Research, vol. 13. New York: Plenum Press.

Anderson, D., D. Lime, and T. Wang. 1998. *Maintaining the quality of park resources and visitor experiences: A handbook for managers.* St. Paul, MN: Cooperative Park Studies Unit, Department of Forest Resources, University of Minnesota.

Clarke, J.N., and D. McCool. 1996. *Staking out the terrain: Power differentials among natural resource management agencies.* 2nd ed. Albany, NY: State University of New York Press.

Cole, C.A., T.L. Serfass, M.C. Brittingham, and R.P. Brooks. 1996. *Managing your restored wetlands.* University Park, PA: Cooperative Extension, The Pennsylvania State University.

Colfer, C., and Y. Byron, eds. 2001. *People managing forests: The links between human well-being and sustainability.* Washington, DC: Resources for the Future.

Cooper, R.B. 1999. *Campground management.* 2nd ed. Champaign, IL: Sagamore Publishing.

Cordell, H.K., principal investigator. 1999. *Outdoor recreation in American life: A national assessment of demand and supply trends.* Champaign, IL: Sagamore Publishing.

Cordell, H.K. 2004. *Outdoor recreation for 21st century America.* State College, PA: Venture Publishing.

Cordell, K., ed. 1998. *Outdoor recreation trends in America.* Champaign, IL: Sagamore Publishing.

Cordell, H.K., and J. Bergstrom, eds. 1999. *Integrating social services with ecosystem management.* Champaign, IL: Sagamore Publishing.

Dearden, P., and R. Rollins, eds. 2002. *Parks and protected areas in Canada: Planning and management.* 2nd ed. Don Mills, ON: Oxford University Press.

Dennis, S. 2001. *Natural resources and the informed citizen.* Champaign, IL: Sagamore Publishing.

Douglas, R.W. 2000. *Forest recreation.* 5th ed. Prospect Heights, IL: Waveland Press.

Driver. B.L., et al., eds. 1996. *Nature and the human spirit: Toward an expanded land management ethic.* State College, PA: Venture Publishing.

Ewert, A.W., ed. 1996. *Natural resource management: The human dimension.* Boulder, CO: Westview Press.

Flug, M., and F.A. Klancrik, eds. 1994. *Marinas, parks and recreation developments.* New York: American Society of Civil Engineers.

Freeman, A.M. 2003. *The measurement of environmental and resource values: Theory and methods.* 2nd ed. Washington, DC: Resources for the Future.

Gartner, W., and D. Lime, eds. 2000. *Trends in outdoor recreation, leisure, and tourism.* Wallingford, Oxon, UK: CABI Publishing.

Hammitt, W.E., and D. Cole. 1998. *Wildland recreation, ecology and management.* 2nd ed. New York: Wiley.

Hanley, N., W. Shaw, and R. Wright, eds. 2003. *The new economics of outdoor recreation.* Northampton, MA: Edward Elgar Publishing.

Harmon, D., and A. Putney, eds. 2003. *The full value of parks: From economics to the intangible.* Lanham, MD: Rowman & Littlefield.

Hendee, J.C., and C.P. Dawson. 2002. *Wilderness management.* 3rd ed. Golden, CO: Fulcrum Publishing.

Hutcheson, J., and R. Snow, eds. 1990. *Outdoor recreation policy: Pleasure and preservation.* New York: Greenwood Press.

Ibrahim, H., and K.A. Cordes. 2002. *Outdoor recreation.* 2nd ed. Champaign, IL: Sagamore Publishing.

Jensen, C. 1995. *Outdoor recreation in America.* 5th ed. Champaign, IL: Human Kinetics.

Jubenville, A., and B. Twight. 1993. *Outdoor recreation management: Theory and application.* 3rd ed. State College, PA: Venture Publishing.

Kaplan, R., S. Kaplan, and R. Ryan. 1998. *With people in mind: Design and management of everyday nature.* Washington, DC: Island Press.

Kaufman, P.W. 1996. *National parks and the woman's voice: A history.* Albuquerque, NM: University of New Mexico Press.

Kellert, S.R., and T.J. Farnham, eds. 2002. *The good in nature and humanity.* Washington, DC: Island Press.

Knight, R.L., and K.J. Gutzwiller, eds. 1995. *Wildlife and recreationists.* Washington, DC: Island Press.

Knight, R.L., and P.B. Landres. 1998. *Stewardship across boundaries.* Washington, DC: Island Press.

Knight, R.L., and S.F. Bates, eds. 1995. *A new century for natural resources management.* Washington, DC: Island Press.

Loomis, J. 1994. *Integrated public lands management.* New York: Columbia University Press.

Loomis, J.B., and R.G. Walsh. 1997. *Recreation economic decisions: Comparing benefits and costs.* 2nd ed. State College, PA: Venture Publishing.

Mackintosh, B. 1991. *The national parks: Shaping the system.* Washington, DC: U.S. Department of the Interior.

Manfredo, M.J., ed. 1992. *Influencing human behavior: Theory and applications in recreation, tourism, and natural resources management.* Champaign, IL: Sagamore Publishing.

Manning, R. 1999. *Studies in outdoor recreation: Search and research for satisfaction.* 2nd ed. Corvallis, OR: Oregon State University Press.

McEwen, D., and C. Mitchell. 1991. *Fundamentals of recreation programming for campgrounds and RV parks.* Champaign, IL: Sagamore Publishing.

Miller, R.W. 1997. *Urban forestry: Planning and managing urban greenspaces.* 2nd ed. Upper Saddle River, NJ: Prentice-Hall.

Mitsch, W.J. and J.G. Gosselink. 1993. *Wetlands.* 2nd ed. New York: Van Nostrand Reinhold.

Moote, M., S. Burke, H. Cortner, and M. Wallace. 1994. *Principles of ecosystem management.* Tucson, AZ: Water Resources Research Center, College of Agriculture, University of Arizona.

Murrell, D.S., and W.O. Dwyer. 1991. *Constitutional law and liability for park law enforcement officers.* 3rd ed. Durham, NC: Carolina Academic Press.

Proceedings of the Fourth International Outdoor Recreation & Tourism Trends Symposium. May 14-17, 1995. St. Paul, MN: University of Minnesota, College of Natural Resources and Minnesota Extension Service.

Rudzitis, G. 1996. *Wilderness and the changing American West.* New York: Wiley.

Runte, A. 1997. *National parks: The American experience.* 3rd ed. Lincoln, NE: University of Nebraska Press.

Runte, A. 1991. *Public lands, public heritage: The national forest idea.* Niwot, CO: Roberts Rinehart.

Sharpe, G.W., C.H. Odegaard, and W.F Sharpe, eds. 1994. *A comprehensive introduction to park management.* 2nd ed. Champaign, IL: Sagamore Publishing.

Sternloff, R., and R. Warren. 1993. *Park and recreation maintenance management.* 3rd ed. Scottsdale, AZ: Publishing Horizons.

Viders, H. 1995. *Marine conservation in the 21st century.* Flagstaff, AZ: Best Publishing.

Vining, J. 1990. *Social science and natural resource recreation management.* Social Behavior and Natural Resource Series. Boulder, CO: Westview Press.

Wagner, F.H., et al. 1995. *Wildlife policies in the national parks.* Washington DC: Island Press.

Wellman, J.D. and D.B. Propst. 2004. *Wildland recreation policy.* 2nd ed. Malabar, FL: Krieger Publishing.

West, P.C., and S.R. Brechin, eds. 1991. *Resident peoples and national parks: Social dilemmas and strategies in international conservation.* Tucson, AZ: University of Arizona Press.

Woudstra, J., and K. Fieldhouse, eds. 2000. *The regeneration of public parks.* London and New York: Published jointly by the Garden History Society, Landscape Design Trust, and E & FN Spon, with support from English Heritage.

Zinser, C.I. 1995. *Outdoor recreation: United States national parks, forests, and public lands.* New York: Wiley.

OUTDOOR AND ENVIRONMENT-RELATED PROGRAMS

This section includes resources on interpretation, environmental education, camping, and adventure programs. It does not include resources for sports played outdoors, nature guides, or activities. See also the section on Therapeutic Recreation, on page 119, or the section on Natural Resource–Based Recreation Management and Policy on page 133.

Agricultural Communicators in Education. 2000. *The communicator's handbook.* 4th ed. Gainesville, FL: Maupin House.

Ajango, D. 2000. *Lessons learned: A guide to accident prevention and crisis response.* Anchorage, AK: Alaska Outdoor and Experiential Education, University of Alaska Anchorage.

Ames, K., B. Franco, and L.T. Frye. 1992. *Ideas and images: Developing interpretive history exhibits.* Thousand Oaks, CA: AltaMira Press.

Ball, A., and B. Ball. 2004. *Basic camp management: An introduction to camp administration.* 6th ed. Martinsville, IN: American Camping Association.

Beck, L., and T. Cable. 2002. *Interpretation for the 21st century.* Champaign, IL: Sagamore Publishing.

Brannan, S., et al. 2003. *Including youth with disabilities in outdoor programs.* Champaign, IL: Sagamore Publishing.

Brochu, L., and T. Merriman. 2002. *Personal interpretation.* Ft. Collins, CO: Interp Press.

Bynum, J.W., K.J. Dowd, and G.M. Roswal. 1997. *Including people with disabilities in camp programs.* Martinsville, IN: American Camping Association.

Byrd, N.J. 1998. *The nature center handbook.* Institute of Museum and Library Services series, 1. Dayton, OH: Association of Nature Center Administrators.

Cloutier, R. 2000. *Legal liability and risk management in adventure tourism.* Kamloops, BC: Bhudak Consultants Ltd.

Coutellier, C. 2004. *Day camp from day one: A hands-on guide for day camp administrators.* Martinsville, IN: American Camping Association.

Davis-Berman, J., and D.S. Berman. 1994. *Wilderness therapy: Foundations, theory, and research.* Dubuque, IA: Kendall/Hunt.

Dougherty, N.J. 1998. *Outdoor recreation safety.* Reston, VA: American Alliance for Health, Physical Education, Recreation and Dance

Driver, B.L., et al., eds. 1996. *Nature and the human spirit: Toward an expanded land management ethic.* State College, PA: Venture Publishing.

Ellmo, W., and J. Graser. 1995. *Adapted adventure activities.* Dubuque, IA: Kendall/Hunt.

Frank, L.S. 2001. *The caring classroom: Using adventure to create community in the classroom and beyond.* Madison, WI: GOAL Consulting.

Freeman, G.J., R.D. Hoy, and K.T. Ricker. 1996. *Unlimited classrooms: A resource guide for inclusive environmental education.* Ashley. OH: Recreation Unlimited, National Challenge Center for People with Disabilities.

Ford P., and J. Blanchard. 1993. *Leadership and administration of outdoor pursuits.* 2nd ed. State College, PA: Venture Publishing.

Gass, M.A. 1993. A*dventure therapy: Therapeutic applications of adventure programming.* Dubuque, IA: Kendall/Hunt.

Gass, M., ed. 1998. *Administrative practices of accredited adventure programs.* Needham Heights, MA: Simon & Schuster Custom Publishing.

Gross, M., and R. Zimmerman. 2002. *Interpretive centers: The history, design, and development of nature and visitor centers.* Interpretive Handbook Series, vol. 5. Steven's Point, WI: University of Wisconsin Press.

Ham, S.H. 1992. *Environmental interpretation.* Golden, CO: North American Press.

Havens, M.D. 1992. *Bridges to accessibility: A primer for including persons with disabilities in adventure curricula.* Hamilton, MA: Project Adventure.

Heintzman, J. 1988. *Making the right connections: A guide for nature writers.* Interpretive Handbook Series, vol. 1. Steven's Point, WI: University of Wisconsin Press.

Hopkins, D., and R. Putnam. 1993. *Personal growth through adventure.* London: David Fulton Publishers.

Kahn, P.H., and S.R. Kellert, eds. 2002. *Children and nature: Psychological, sociocultural, and evolutionary investigations.* Cambridge, MA: MIT Press.

Kaplan, R., and S. Kaplan. 1989. *The experience of nature: A psychological perspective.* New York: Cambridge University Press.

Kaplan, R., S. Kaplan, and R.L. Ryan. 1998. *With people in mind: Design and management of everyday nature.* Washington, DC: Island Press.

Knudson, D.M., T.T. Cable, and L. Beck. 2003. *Interpretation of cultural and natural resources.* 2nd ed. State College, PA: Venture Publishing.

Kraft, R.J., and J. Kielsmeier, eds. 1995. *Experiential learning in schools and higher education.* Dubuque, IA: Kendall/Hunt.

Lais, G.J., et al. 1993. *Integrated outdoor educational and adventure programs.* Champaign, IL: Sagamore Publishing.

Machlis, G.E., and D.R. Field. 1992. *On interpretation: Sociology for interpreters of natural and cultural history.* Rev. ed. Corvallis, OR: Oregon State University Press.

Marshall, I. 2003. *Peak experiences: Walking meditations on leisure, nature, and need.* Charlottesville, VA: University of Virginia Press.

Matthews, B.E., and C.K. Riley. 1995. *Outdoor ethics education programs.* Vienna, VA: National Wildlife Federation.

Meier, J.F., and V. Mitchell. 1993. *Camp counseling.* 7th ed. Dubuque, IA: Brown & Benchmark.

Miles, J.C., and S. Priest. eds. 1998. *Adventure education.* 2nd ed. State College, PA: Venture Publishing.

Miles, J.C., and S. Priest, eds. 1999. *Adventure programming.* State College, PA: Venture Publishing.

Nadler, R.S., and J.L. Luckner. 1992. *Processing the adventure experience.* Dubuque, IA: Kendall/Hunt.

National Therapeutic Recreation Society (NTRS) and National Recreation and Park Association (NRPA). 2001. *Best of outdoor adventure programming in therapeutic recreation.* Ashburn, VA: National Recreation and Park Association.

Nebbe, L.L. 1991. *Nature as a guide: Using nature in counseling, therapy, and education.* Minneapolis: Educational Media.

Ogilvie, K. 1993. *Leading and managing groups in the outdoors.* Sheffield, UK: NAOE Publications.

Panicucci, J. 2002. *Middle school: Adventure curriculum for physical education.* Beverly, MA: Project Adventure.

Panicucci, J. 2003. *High school: Adventure curriculum for physical education.* Beverly, MA: Project Adventure.

Priest, S., and M.A. Gass. 1997. *Effective leadership in adventure programming.* Champaign, IL: Human Kinetics.

Regnier, K., M. Gross, and R. Zimmerman. 1992. *The interpreter's guidebook: Techniques for programs and presentations.* Interpretive Handbook Series, vol. 2. Steven's Point, WI: University of Wisconsin Press.

Rohnke, K., and S. Butler. 1995. *QuickSilver: Adventure games, initiative problems, trust activities, and a guide to effective leadership.* Dubuque, IA: Kendall/Hunt.

Rohwedder, R. 1990. *Computer-aided environmental education.* Troy, OH: North American Association for Environmental Education.

Roland, C.C., R.J. Wagner, and R.J. Weigand. 1995. *Do it . . . and understand, the bottom line on corporate experiential learning.* Dubuque, IA: Kendall/Hunt.

Schleien, S., et al. 1993. *Integrated outdoor education and adventure programs.* Champaign, IL: Sagamore Publishing.

Schoel, J., and R.S. Maizell. 2002. *Exploring islands of healing: New perspectives on adventure-based counseling.* Beverly, MA: Project Adventure.

Smith, T.E., et al. 1992. *The theory and practice of challenge education.* Dubuque, IA: Kendall/Hunt.

Smolowe, A., et al. 1999. *Adventure in business.* Needham Heights, MA: Pearson Custom Publishing. *A publication of Project Adventure.*

Trapp, S., M. Gross, and R. Zimmerman. 1994. *Signs, trails and wayside exhibits: Connecting people and places.* 2nd ed. Interpretive Handbook Series, vol. 4. Steven's Point, WI: University of Wisconsin Press.

Veverka, J.A. 1994. *Interpretive master planning.* Helena, MT: Falcon Press Publishing.

Warren, K., M. Sakofs, and J.S. Hunt, Jr., eds. 1995. *The theory of experiential education.* Dubuque, IA: Kendall/Hunt.

Webster, S.E. 1989. *Ropes course safety manual.* Dubuque, IA: Kendall/Hunt.

Wisconsin Department of Public Instruction. 1994. *Curriculum guide in environmental education.* Madison, WI: Wisconsin Department of Public Instruction.

Zehr, J., M. Gross, and R. Zimmerman. 1992. *Creating environmental publications: A guide to writing and designing for interpreters and environmental educators.* Interpretive Handbook Series, vol. 3. Steven's Point, WI: University of Wisconsin Press.

CLASSICAL

This category includes books published before 1990; most are out of print, so check your library. This section includes books from nearly all of the functional sections. Some remain a valuable resource, and all provide excellent background perspectives and understanding of the programs and the leadership and their thinking at that time. These writings reflect the historical foundations of the field.

Altman, I., and J.F. Wohlwill. 1983. *Behavior and the natural environment.* Human Behavior and Environment: Advances in Theory and Research, vol. 6. New York: Plenum Press.

Anderson, J. 1958. *Work and leisure.* New York: Glencoe Press.

Avedon, E.M. 1971. *The study of games.* New York: Wiley.

Brightbill, C.K. 1960. *The challenge of leisure.* Englewood Cliffs, NJ: Prentice-Hall.

Brightbill, C.K. 1961. *Man and leisure: A philosophy of recreation.* Englewood Cliffs, NJ: Prentice-Hall.

Brockman, C.F., and L.O. Merriam. 1979. *Recreational use of wildlands.* 3rd ed. New York: McGraw-Hill.

Brown, W.E. 1971. *Islands of hope.* Washington, DC: National Recreation and Park Association.

Butler, G. 1976. *Introduction to community recreation.* 5th ed. New York: McGraw-Hill.

Cabot, R.C. 1914. *What men live by.* New York: Houghton Mifflin.

Caillos, R. 1961. *Man, play, and games.* 2nd ed. New York: McGraw-Hill.

Campbell, D.T., and J.C. Stanley. 1963. *Experimental and quasi-experimental designs for research.* Chicago: Rand McNally.

Cheek, N.H., Jr., D.R. Field, and R.J. Burdge. 1976. *Leisure and recreation places.* Ann Arbor, MI: Ann Arbor Science.

Cheek, N.H., Jr., and W.R. Burch, Jr. 1976. *The social organization of leisure in human society.* New York: Harper and Row.

Chubb, M., and H.R. Chubb. 1981. *One-third of our time: An introduction to recreation behavior and resources.* New York: Wiley.

Clawson, M., and J. Knetsh. 1966. *Economics of outdoor recreation.* Baltimore: Johns Hopkins University Press.

Csikszentmihalyi, M. 1975. *Beyond boredom and anxiety.* San Francisco: Jossey-Bass.

Csikszentmihalyi, M., and I.S. Csikszentmihalyi, ed. 1988. *Optimal experience: Psychological studies of flow in consciousness.* New York: Cambridge University Press.

Curtis, H.S. 1971. *The play movement and its significance.* New York: Macmillan.

Curtis, H.S. 1914. *Play and recreation.* Boston: Ginn.

Dare, B., G. Welton, and W. Coe. 1987. *Concepts of leisure in western thought: A critical and historical analysis.* Dubuque, IA: Kendall/Hunt.

deGrazia, S. 1964. *Of time, work, and leisure.* Garden City, NY: Doubleday.

Doell, C.E., and G.B. Fitzgerald. 1954. *A brief history of parks and recreation in the United States.* Chicago: Athletic Institute.

Doell, C.E., and L.F. Twardzik. 1979. *Elements of park and recreation administration.* 4th ed. Minneapolis: Burgess.

Donaldson, G.W., and O. Goering. 1972. *Perspectives on outdoor education . . . readings.* Dubuque, IA: Brown.

Dulles, F.R. 1965. *A history of recreation: America learns to play.* 2nd ed. Englewood Cliffs, NJ: Prentice-Hall.

Dumazedier, J. 1974. *The sociology of leisure.* Amsterdam: Elsevier.

Eells, E. 1986. *Eleanor Eell's history of organized camping: The first 100 years.* Martinsville, IN: American Camping Association.

Ellis, M.J. 1973. *Why people play.* Englewood Cliffs, NJ: Prentice-Hall.

Freeberg, W.H., and L.E. Taylor. 1961. *Philosophy of outdoor education.* Minneapolis: Burgess.

Freeberg, W.H., and L.E. Taylor. 1963. *Programs in outdoor education.* Minneapolis: Burgess.

Gold, S.M. 1973. *Urban recreation planning.* Philadelphia: Lea & Febiger.

Good, A.H. 1938, reprinted 1999. *Park and recreation structures.* New York: Princeton Architectural Press.

    Originally published by the National Park Service in three parts: Part I, Administration and Basic Facilities; Part II, Recreational and Cultural Facilities; Part III, Overnight and Organized Camp Facilities.

Goodale, T.L., and G.C. Godbey. 1988. *The evolution of leisure: Historical and philosophical perspectives.* State College, PA: Venture Publishing.

Gray, D., and D.A. Pelegrino. 1973. *Reflections on the recreation and park movement.* Dubuque, IA: Brown.

Gulick, L.H. 1920. *A philosophy of play.* New York: Scribner's.

Hammerman, D.R., and W.M. Hammerman. 1973. *Teaching in the outdoors.* Minneapolis: Burgess.

Hjelte, G., and J.S. Shivers. 1978. *Public administration of recreational services.* 2nd ed. Philadelphia: Lea & Febiger.

Howard, D., and J. Crompton. 1980. *Financing, managing, and marketing recreation and park resources.* Dubuque, IA: Brown.

Huizinga, J. 1950. *Homo Ludens: A study of the play element in culture.* Boston: Beacon Press.

Iso-Ahola, S.E. 1980. *The social psychology of leisure and recreation.* Dubuque, IA: Brown.

Jacks, L.P. 1932. *Education through recreation.* New York: Harper & Brothers.

Kaplan, M. 1960. *Leisure in America: A social inquiry.* New York: Wiley.

Kaplan, M. 1975. *Leisure: Theory and policy.* New York: Wiley.

Kaplan, M., and P. Bosserman, eds. 1971. *Technology, human values and leisure.* New York: Abingdon Press.

Kelly, J.R. 1987. *Freedom to be: A new sociology of leisure.* New York: Macmillan.

Kleemeier, R.W., ed. 1961. *Aging and leisure.* New York: Oxford University Press.

Knapp, R.F., and C.E. Hartsoe. 1979. *Play for America: The National Recreation Association 1906-1965.* Alexandria, VA: National Recreation and Park Association.

Lancaster, R.A., ed. 1983. *Recreation, park and open space standards and guidelines.* Ashburn, VA: National Recreation and Park Association.

Larrabee, E., and R. Meyersohn, eds. 1958. *Mass leisure.* Glencoe, IL: Free Press.

Lee, J. 1916. *Play in education.* New York: Macmillan.

Lee, R. 1964. *Religion and leisure in America.* Nashville: Abingdon Press.

Leopold, A. 1966. *Sand County almanac.* New York: Oxford University Press

    Many editions have been published by various organizations, e.g., 1974 Sierra Club. The original date of 1949 was copyrighted by Oxford University Press.

Lewis, W.J. 1980. *Interpreting for park visitors.* Philadelphia: Eastern Acorn Press.

Linder, S.B. 1970. *The harried leisure class.* New York: Columbia University Press.

Loughmiller, C. 1965. *Wilderness road.* Austin, TX: Hogg Foundation for Mental Health, University of Texas.

Loughmiller, C. 1979. *Kids in trouble.* Tyler, TX: Wildwood Books.

Manley, H., and M.F. Drury. 1952. *Education through school camping.* St. Louis: Mosby.

Meier, J.F., T.W. Morash, and G.E. Welton, eds. 1987. *High-adventure outdoor pursuits: Organization and leadership.* 2nd ed. Columbus, OH: Publishing Horizons.

Miller, N.P., and D.M. Robinson. 1963. *The leisure age: Its challenge to recreation.* Belmont, CA: Wadsworth.

Murphy, J., 1981. *Concepts of leisure: Philosophical implications.* Englewood Cliffs, NJ: Prentice-Hall.

Nash, J.B. 1953. *Philosophy of recreation and leisure.* Dubuque, IA: Brown.

Nash, J.B. 1965. *Recreation: Pertinent readings.* Dubuque, IA: Brown.

Nash, R.F. 1982. *Wilderness and the American mind.* 3rd ed. New Haven, CT: Yale University Press.

Neulinger, J. 1983. *The psychology of leisure.* 2nd ed. Springfield, IL: C.C. Thomas.

Overstreet, H.A. 1934. *A guide to civilized loafing.* New York: Norton

Parker, S. 1983. *Leisure and work.* Leisure and Recreation Studies, vol. 2. London: Allen and Unwin.

Peiper, J. 1963. *Leisure: The basis of culture.* New York: Mentor-Omega Books.

Rainwater, C.E. 1922. *The play movement in the United States.* Chicago: University of Chicago Press.

Romney, G.E. 1972. *Off the job living: A modern concept of recreation and its place in the postwar world.* Salem, NH: Ayer.

Smith, D.A., and N. Theberge. 1987. *Why people recreate: An overview of research.* Champaign, IL: Life Enhancement Publication.

Smith, J.W., R.E. Carlson, H.B. Masters, and G.W. Donaldson. n.d. *Outdoor education.* 2nd ed. Englewood Cliffs, NJ: Prentice-Hall.

Staley, E.J., and N.P. Miller, eds. 1972. *Leisure and the quality of life.* Washington, DC: American Association of Health, Physical Education and Recreation.

Suchman, E.A. 1967. *Evaluative research: Principles and practice in public service and social action programs.* New York: Russell Sage Foundation.

Tilden, F. 1977. *Interpreting our heritage.* 3rd ed. Chapel Hill, NC: University of North Carolina Press.

Van Matre, S. 1972. *Acclimatizing: A personal and reflective approach to a natural relationship.* Martinsville, IN: American Camping Association.

Van Matre, S. 1972. *Acclimatization: A sensory and conceptual approach to ecological involvement.* Martinsville, IN: American Camping Association.

Veblen, T. 1963. *The theory of the leisure class: An economic study of institutions.* New York: New American Library.

Wade, M.G., ed. 1985. *Constraints on leisure.* Springfield, IL: Charles C. Thomas.

Weir, L. 1928. *Parks: A manual of municipal and county parks.* New York: National Recreation Association.

Wilson, T.B., et al. 1979. *An introduction to industrial recreation.* Dubuque, IA: Brown.

SELECTED PROFESSIONAL AND RESEARCH PERIODICALS

Periodicals, both journals and newsletters, contain the most up-to-date reporting of what's happening in the professional field. You should regularly read those in your specific field of interest. The periodicals listed here are categorized similarly to the categories in parts II and III.

Some of the periodicals are official publications of a professional organization or trade association. Part III lists the publications of the respective organizations. Other periodicals are sponsored by an industry that serves the profession, such as fitness and athletic management; an organization or agency that serves a special interest, such as the environment; or a publisher that focuses on a certain topic, such as research. Keep alert to changes in publications, discontinuance or new ones, and change of name, format, or frequency.

Most of the organizations include a subscription to their periodicals in the membership fee. Many publications can be found online, especially newsletters. Periodicals from related fields usually are available at college or university libraries, but be aware that libraries pay considerably more for an institution subscription than a person does for an individual subscription, and in a budget crunch, libraries may limit their number of subscriptions.

One way to peruse the contents of current journals in related fields is through *Current Contents,* which prints weekly the table of contents of hundreds of journals. Most college and university libraries subscribe; it is available in hard copy and online (www.isinet.com/products/cap/ccc/). Although each issue includes a topical index, you should scan the article titles listed in the actual table of contents. This will yield many topics of interest you would not find using only the index.

Although support organizations, such as The Nature Conservancy, Defenders of Wildlife, Sierra Club, or National Wildlife Association, and special interest organizations, such as American Water Ski Association, National Alliance for Youth Sports, National Rifle Association, and American Folklore Society produce many useful journals and newsletters, the listing here focuses only on recreation and park professional periodicals and selected related fields pertinent to the specific category.

Natural Resources and Environment (general)

Agricultural Experiment Stations (state land-grant university) publications
Environment & Behavior
Environmental Ethics
Human Dimensions of Wildlife
ILVS: A Journal of Visitor Behavior
Journal of Wilderness
Natural Resources & Environment
Society and Natural Resources
Trends
USFS Experiment Stations "Recent Reports"
Research
Women in Natural Resources

Interpretation (natural, cultural, and underwater)

History News
InterpEdge
Interpscan
Journal of Interpretation Research
Legacy
The Interpreter
Visitor Studies Today

Environmental Education, Adventure Programs, Camping, and Outdoor Recreation

Adventure Education
CCI Journal
Camp Business
Camp Management
Camping Magazine
Connect
Current, the Journal of Marine Education
Environmental Education Research

Journal of Environmental Education

Journal of Experiential Education

Taproot

The Outdoor Network

Update (Outdoor education research news, published by Outdoor Education Research & Evaluation Center, University of NH)

Therapeutic Recreation, Aging, and Disabilities

Access Today

Adapted Physical Activity Quarterly

EP (Exceptional Parent) Magazine

Journal of Aging and Health

Journal of Aging & Physical Activity

Journal of Leisurability

Palaestra

Research on Aging

Strides Magazine

Therapeutic Recreation Journal

Commercial Recreation and Tourism and Employee Recreation

Anatolia, an International Journal of Tourism & Hospitality Research

Annals of Tourism

Annals of Tourism Research

Club Industry

Employee Services Magazine

Event Management

Festival Management & Event Tourism

Health Club Management

Journal of Hospitality & Leisure Marketing

Journal of Hospitality and Tourism Research

Journal of International Hospitality, Leisure & Tourism Management

Journal of Sport Tourism

Journal of Tourism and Hospitality Marketing

Journal of Travel and Tourism Marketing

Journal of Travel Research

Journal of Vacation Marketing

Leisure Management, Leisure Opportunities

Resort and Commercial Recreation

Review of Tourism Research

Tourism Management

Tourism Recreation Research

Recreation and Parks

Journal of Physical Education, Recreation & Dance (JOPERD)

Journal of Applied Recreation Research

Journal of Leisure Research

Journal of Park and Recreation Administration

Leisure, Recreation & Tourism Abstracts

Leisure Resource Management Quarterly

Leisure Sciences

Leisure Studies

Park Maintenance

Parks & Recreation
Parks and Recreation Business
Public Administration Review
Recreation Resources
Schole: A Journal of Leisure Studies and Recreation Education
Society and Leisure
State Journals—California, Illinois, North Carolina, Pennsylvania
Visions in Leisure and Business
World Leisure Journal

Nonprofit Sector and Behavioral Sciences

American Sociological Review
American Behavioral Scientist
Child & Youth Care Forum
Evaluation and Program Planning
Journal of Adolescence Research
Journal of Health and Social Behavior
Journal of Nonprofit and Public Sector Marketing
New Designs for Youth Development
Nonprofit Management & Leadership
Nonprofit World
Social Psychology Quarterly

Research and Evaluation

Abstracts from Symposium on Leisure Research (Held annually by NRPA Congress.)
Action Research
AERJ: American Educational Research Journal
Applied Psychological Measurement
Dissertation Abstracts
Educational and Psychological Measurement
Educational Researcher
Evaluating Review
Evaluation and Program Planning
Field Methods
Future Survey
Journal of Educational and Behavioral Statistics
Leisure, Recreation and Tourism Abstracts
Organizational Research Methods
QI: Qualitative Inquiry
RER: Review of Educational Research
SMR: Sociological Methods and Research

In addition, many abstracting services are available in the library.

Sport, Athletics, and Recreational Sport

Athletic Business
Athletic Management
Aquatics International
International Journal of Sport Sociology
Journal of Health, Physical Education and Recreation
Journal of Sport & Exercise Psychology
Journal of Sport & Exercise Science (With supplement of abstracts of completed research.)

Journal of Sport & Social Issues
Journal of Sport Management
Recreational Sports and Fitness
Recreational Sports Journal
Research Quarterly for Exercise & Sport (With supplement of abstracts of completed research.)
Sport and Social Issues
Sport Marketing Quarterly
Strategies
The Physician and Sportsmedicine
Women in Sport & Physical Activity Journal

Newsletters

Federal Parks & Recreation
Human Dimensions in Wildlife Newsletter
Leisure Industry Report
Management Strategy
Outdoor News Bulletin
Park Science
Recreation Access in the 90s
Recreation Executive Report
Research Digest (President's Council on Physical Fitness & Sports)
Travel & Tourism

See also professional organization newsletters in part III

Legal Periodicals

Community Risk Management Insurance
From the Gym to the Jury
Hospitality Law
Journal of Legal Aspects of Sport
Legal Aspects of Sport & Physical Activity Newsletter
Liability and Immunity (Local Government Research Group)
Mental & Physical Disability Law Reporter
Municipal Litigation Reporter
Outdoor Education and Recreation Law Quarterly
Personnel Law Update
Perspective (campus)
Premises Liability Reporter
Recreation & Parks Law Reporter
The Exercise Standards & Malpractice Reporter
Sports and the Courts
Sports, Parks, and Recreation Law Reporter

Proceedings

Coalition for Education in the Outdoors Research Symposium (1996) Interpretive Sourcebook (NAI)
Northeastern Recreation Research Symposium (NRRS)
Outdoor Recreation & Tourism Trends Symposium

Selected Papers From the NAAEE Annual Conference

Symposium on Social Aspects and Recreation Research

See also organizations issuing proceedings in part III.

References

Commission for Accreditation of Park and Recreation Agencies. 2001. *Self-assessment manual for quality operation of park and recreation agencies.* Ashburn, VA: National Recreation and Park Association.

DePauw, K.P., and S.J. Gavron. 2005. *Disability and sport.* 2nd ed. Champaign, IL: Human Kinetics.

Edginton, Christopher, et al. 2004. *Leisure programming.* New York: McGraw-Hill.

Hawkins, B.A. (ed). 1998. *Historical Perspectives on the Development of the NRPA Council on Accreditation.* Ashburn, VA: National Recreation and Parks Association.

Schein, E.H., and D.W. Kommers. 1972. *Professional education: Some new directions.* New York: McGraw-Hill Book Company.

van der Smissen, B. 2004. "Standards and Accreditation" in Edginton, C., (ed). *Papers of the American leisure academy.* Cedar Falls, IA: University of Northern Iowa, School of HPELS.

van der Smissen, B., M. Moiseichik, and V. Hartenburg, eds. 2005. *Management of park and recreation.* 2nd ed. Ashburn, VA: National Recreation and Parks Association.

About the Author

Betty van der Smissen, ReD, JD, is professor emeritus of recreation and parks at Michigan State University and visiting professor in the Division of Leisure, Youth, and Human Services at the University of Northern Iowa. As a professional, she believes in active participation for enhancement of the profession. As an educator, she believes that students should acquire knowledge of the various professional organizations in the field. Thus, Dr. van der Smissen has maintained memberships in many organizations and has been active in the fields of recreation, camping, environmental education, and adventure and challenge for nearly 50 years. The national organizations in these and several related fields have recognized Dr. van der Smissen's professional contributions by honoring her with their highest awards for service as well as naming certain awards in recognition of her service. These include a leadership award, a research grant, and a conference scholarship. Dr. van der Smissen has been elected to membership in the principal academies of her profession. As a lawyer and a member of the American Bar Association, she has contributed her time through presentations at conferences, workshops, and other meetings and has written about legal liability and risk management. The American Bar Association has recognized her service with its Vanguard Award for lifetime contribution to nonprofit organizations.

Dr. van der Smissen is noted for her extensive work, beginning in the early 1960s and continuing to date, in the development, implementation, and revision of the four major accreditation programs in her fields: academic curriculum, organized camping, adventure and challenge programs, and recreation and park agencies. She has served more than one term on the national accreditation body (council commission board) of each of these four programs. Dr. van der Smissen believes that through the accreditation standards, the professionalism and quality of programs and services are greatly enhanced, and thus the profession is enhanced.